STOCK MARKET
INVESTING
FOR BEGINNERS

**THE EASIEST GUIDE TO LEARN THE BASICS OF THE STOCK
MARKET, START CREATING YOUR WEALTH AND PURSUE
FINANCIAL FREEDOM WITH PROVEN STRATEGIES**

JAMES JOHNSON

Stock Market Investing for Beginners:

The EASIEST GUIDE to Learn the BASICS of Stock Market, Start Creating Your WEALTH and Pursue Financial Freedom with Proven STRATEGIES

James Johnson

Table of Contents

Introduction

Congratulations and welcome to *Stock Market Investing for Beginners*. In this short but informative guide, we hope to give you the knowledge that will empower you to take control of your own financial future!

Stock market investing provides an unprecedented way to grow your income and wealth. In this book, we will introduce you to the stock market and show you how to invest efficiently and effectively, using time-tested strategies that will help to minimize your risk. Most people set up a 401k or IRA and don't give any further thought to their retirement plans. In this book, we will dive into managing your portfolio yourself so that you – and not some paid advisor – can direct where your portfolio goes, apply your own investment strategies, and pick investments that you believe will grow your income and wealth.

In this book, we will cover everything you need to know in order to get started. We will explain what to look for when buying stocks and show you how to trade online, using some exciting commission free opportunities with mobile apps. We will also explore different ways you can get into stocks, including buying individual stocks, exchange-traded funds, and mutual funds. Then we'll enter the world of bond investing and not only see how you can invest in bonds, but we'll look at ways to leverage the stock market to do it. Then we'll discuss mutual funds and give you the information you need in order to weigh whether or not they are worth it for your situation.

We'll also discuss more advanced techniques such as options trading, day trading, and swing trading. Finally, we'll review some common beginners' mistakes to help you mitigate your own risks.

Thank you for downloading this book. I hope that you find it informative and that it helps you build your own highly profitable portfolio!

Chapter 1

Introduction to the Stock Market

If you surveyed the general public, you would find that most people have a vague sense of what the stock market is, but few truly understand it. In this book, our goal is to present the ins and outs of the stock market and investing so that you have a rigorous understanding of the markets and how they work. At the same time, we're going to present everything at the level of a beginner. We'll use simple language as much as possible while familiarizing you with the lingo. No math background is required, even though high-level math lies behind many of the tools used by traders. All you need is some basic knowledge and a dose of some common sense. Before I go on, I want to congratulate you. By downloading this book, you have demonstrated that you aren't someone who acts on a whim. You are willing to learn and prepare before throwing all of your money at something. And that is very important. While the stock market offers unlimited opportunities and can help you to build substantial wealth, it's not gambling, nor is it a game or a guarantee. There are real risks, and protecting yourself against the risks is the smart strategy. That is done first by having knowledge.

To get started, we're going to familiarize ourselves with what the stock market actually is and where it came from. We're also going to discuss some of the different ways that people handle investing, from mutual funds to day trading. In this chapter, we will only provide a quick introduction to each investing style; we will use later chapters to explore them in detail. Finally, we'll examine some "what if" scenarios and success stories. No matter which path you choose, I wish you happy investing!

Why Does Wall Street Exist in the First Place?

The answer is painstakingly obvious, but few people on the street could answer this question. Wall Street exists for the same reason that banks exist. Some people have money, or *capital*, while others have ideas and companies, but they lack the capital they need to build them out and earn a profit. Markets are simply a meeting place to bring all these people together so they can make a mutually beneficial exchange. Markets started out small and direct, with people meeting face to face. Times have changed, and now markets have grown into the modern versions we see today, large and often completely automated with computer-directed trades. But at the lowest levels, the fundamentals are the same as they were hundreds of years ago as are the reasons the markets exist.

In a capitalist society, many people earn more money than they need to satisfy their basic wants. And its human nature to want more of what you have, and those of us who are forward thinking like to plan for the future when we may not be able to work because of old age or disability. So, in order to grow their own capital and invest in the future people with the money available to do so are interested in investing it in order to see a return. That return can be long-term to build their wealth and secure their future, or it could be short-term to earn a profit.

People who create ideas for new products or start businesses, on the other hand, desperately need the money. They are willing to pay others that have it in return for the ability to use the capital in their business. As we will see, there are different ways that this arrangement can be accomplished.

A quick review of the history of finance

The stock market didn't appear out of thin air, and there hasn't always been a stock market. So where did it come from?

The ideas of finance and investing have slowly developed over the centuries. We could go back all the way to ancient times and investigate the invention of money and the earliest hints of trading, but modern finance actually began developing during the Middle Ages in Europe. The impetus for this development came mainly from the many trade fairs that began popping up across the continent during the early Middle Ages. The first trade fairs began developing around the year 1000 AD and thereafter.

In those days people had to have direct personal contact in order to trade goods. So, a purveyor of spices or fabrics had to meet other merchants or prospective customers in person in order to sell the goods. One problem people had in the middle ages was that travel was relatively dangerous and took a long time. You could either trade locally or spend a great deal of time traveling (and risking both your personal safety and the theft of your wares), and neither option was that appealing. The advent of the trade fairs was a complete game changer. People could gather at major trade fairs and exchange their goods, eliminating the problems cited using the other ways of reaching customers.

Other things that stifled trade at the time were high rates of taxation and border duties. However, the powers that be allowed merchants to trade at the fairs while being exempt to most of the fees that were around at the time. Places that had the best deals ended up seeing the most economic growth and development. This was a large boost to the development and popularity of the trade fairs.

The city of Antwerp in Belgium became a free trade zone. Many merchants relocated there permanently, which altered the course of history for the city, and for finance in general. We can see the earliest glimmerings of Wall Street in these developments.

One of the most interesting developments that occurred with the trade fairs were merchants that traded in money itself. With merchants possibly joining the fairs from multiple kingdoms or nations, the currency exchange was necessary. Thus, the first Forex markets were born. In addition, money merchants also provided loans.

Later in the book, we will closely examine the notion of a bond, which is essentially a loan of capital in exchange for interest. The idea of a municipal bond, that is a bond sold by a local or city government, was developed in Italy in the 1200s-1600s. Buyers of the bond would receive interest payments from the government entity in exchange for the principal loaned for the bond. Early bonds were perpetual, so you would essentially give your money away in exchange for an endless stream of interest payments (endless that is, until you passed away). In later centuries the idea of a perpetual bond was replaced by a bond with a maturity date, that is the principal would be returned at an agreed upon date in the future ending the bond contract.

Other developments that occurred during the middle ages included the concept of an annuity or a perpetual fixed payment. We will discuss annuities later in the book.

The idea of selling *stock* in a company arose during the age of exploration in Europe. For the first time, companies began to grow so large and so rapidly that they could not be financed without seeking access to public capital. We call this type of investing equity investing, to distinguish it from bonds. Equity means that you own a *share* of the company. The purpose of equity investing is to make a profit, or *capital gain* (literally to gain more capital than you originally had). The first instance of equity financing was the creation of the Dutch East India company. You could buy a stake in this company (stock) in exchange for a share of the companies' profits.

Soon after this concept was developed, human nature took over. What are you going to do when you own a profitable object? Some people will hold it hoping to enjoy the long-term fruits of the company, but others are going to sell their share, hoping to make an immediate profit. Thus, the first stock markets were born, in the city of Amsterdam.

It's not a coincidence that the New York Stock Exchange started on Wall Street, a location that was once owned by the Dutch. However, that didn't happen until the late 19th century. Now that we know where the stock market comes from, we can start discussing what we need to know about it in order to invest.

Types of Investing and Definitions

The modern world of stock markets has been in place for quite some time. Although some of the details have changed and the methods of trading have been advanced through the use of technology, the basic concepts are the same as they were when people were buying and selling shares in the Dutch East India company. We will explore the main ways you can invest your money in future chapters of the book, but in this introduction, we are going to list them here with some introductory comments.

Stocks

You can buy a share of ownership in a company by purchasing shares of stock. On the stock market, stocks are often distinguished in different ways, such as how old the company is, how large the company is, and its profitability. Investors can use stocks for different investment goals based on the company's performance and growth. For example, you might want stability with long term, sustainable growth, or you may opt for rapid, short-term growth.

Publicly Traded Company

When you think of the stock market, you're thinking of a publicly traded company. And that is the focus of this book. A publicly traded company is one that sells shares of stock in the company on a public exchange, like the New York Stock Exchange or NASDAQ, which is a stock exchange developed for high-tech companies. The ownership of a publicly traded company is spread out among members of the general public through the sale of shares of its stock. The shares can be freely traded on a stock exchange. Public trading of stock is heavily regulated, in the United States, this is done by the Securities and Exchange Commission.

In order to buy or sell shares of stock, you have to go through a broker (or *brokerage*) which is a company that buys and sells the stock on the stock market on your behalf (usually for a fee called a *commission*). Some people buy stock to invest in the company, which means you are hoping to make a capital gain on the long-term growth prospects of the company. Investment is also attempting to take advantage of the long-term growth of the economy at large. Over time the stock market grows in size, with individual stocks gaining a lot of value as the years go by. The market trends with the economy, and so it also follows its ups and downs. As we will see later, the downturns aren't really that relevant for long-term investors. Many people waste their energy panicking over recessions and the short-term stock market downturns that accompany them. These are actually buying opportunities.

Other people who buy and sell stock are more accurately described as *traders*, that is they hope to buy and sell stocks over a short time period in order to realize a profit. When you are a trader, you're not an investor but rather using the stock market as a basis for your own for-profit business. Nonetheless, even if you aren't going to become a trader, you can learn a lot by educating yourself about the metrics they use to determine, buy and sell signals for stocks.

Brokerage

As we mentioned earlier, a brokerage is a company that buys and sells stocks on your behalf. A member of the general public doesn't go to the stock exchange and directly buy stocks, you use the brokerage to do it for you. In exchange for this service, most charge a commission. You have probably heard the names of many brokerages such as Charles Schwab. In today's world, you can buy and sell stocks online or even with smartphone apps. Some newer brokerages that have come of age in the past 20 years from changing technology include eTrade, Tasty Trade, and Robinhood.

Liquidity

The term liquidity refers to how quickly you can turn an investment into cash. So, money itself is highly liquid. It is cash! Some given investment X might be more liquid than Y if you can sell X for cash immediately while it might take a long time to sell Y and get the money.

Dividend

A *dividend* is a cash payment made by a company to people who own shares of stocks in the company. Most dividends are paid out on a quarterly basis. Dividends are paid out of profits made by the company. Not all stocks pay dividends. They can be a source of regular income if you buy large amounts of shares, but you have to be aware of what companies pay dividends and which ones don't if that is part of your strategy.

Penny Stocks and Over the Counter Trading

A *penny stock* is what the name implies –it's a stock that is trading for less than five dollars per share (traditionally less than a dollar, thus the term penny – but inflation has changed the relative definition which is set by the SEC). Trading in penny stocks is highly *speculative*. When we say the investment is speculative, that means you're usually investing on a gamble that the price of the instrument will increase in the future and that there is a high risk of loss. It's not surprising that penny stocks are speculative; they are priced low for a reason. These tend to be small companies. Some even trade on the major stock exchanges. Sometimes, companies with penny stocks may be a "hidden gem." For example, the company may be in the development stage of a new product, and so people might be drawn to invest in penny stocks hoping the share price will skyrocket when the product is released. It is often difficult to find buyers of penny stocks, so they are considered illiquid.

Most penny stocks trade "over the counter." That means they are not traded on a stock exchange. Trades are made directly between the buyer and the seller in an unsupervised manner or through dealers. Prices of penny stocks are highly *volatile*, meaning the price per share fluctuates wildly. That is why many speculators buy penny stocks; they hope to profit from the volatility. That is easier said than done for most, however, since it may be difficult to find a buyer when the price goes up (in contrast finding a buyer on a stock exchange is practically automatic).

Historically they were traded with pink pieces of paper, so they are also known as "pink sheets." In short, this is a high-risk activity and not recommended if your goal is an investment and long-term growth.

Initial Public Offering (IPO)

An initial public offering is when a growing company offers shares to the general public on the major stock exchanges for the first time. While they can often be opportunities to "get in on the ground floor" in many cases, the IPO doesn't work out the way people expected, and the stock ends up languishing.

Investment Bank

An example of an investment bank is Goldman-Sachs. Investment banks take part in large financial transactions and can do so with private companies or government securities. They serve as the intermediary between a company that is entering the stock market for the first time with an IPO, and the general public. A law passed during the great depression, Glass-Steagall, used to separate investment banks from ordinary commercial banks that engaged in typical banking activities like maintaining checking and savings accounts and offering loans. However, during the Clinton administration, it was repealed, and today, banks can assume both roles. An example of that type of bank is Bank of America. Some people believe that the repeal of the Glass-Steagal act helped create the 2008 financial crisis.

Bonds

A bond is a loan, but you play the role of the bank and are the one who lends the money. You led your money by purchasing a bond. You can buy bonds from private corporations, small local and city governments, state governments, and even the U.S. government. The money you lend is called the principal, and you are paid interest in exchange for buying the bond, until the maturity date. Bonds last for a certain time period and expire on the maturity date when your principal is returned. Bonds are traded in secondary markets, and many people are bond traders hoping to profit on the fluctuating prices of bonds. The price of a bond changes because of the interest rates paid on bonds changes. We will explore how this occurs and why as we progress through the book. In a future chapter, we will explore ways that a small investor can invest in bonds.

Funds

A fund is a pool of money used to buy shares of stock or other financial instruments. There are two main types of funds, mutual funds, and exchange-traded funds. You can invest indirectly by purchasing shares of the funds. For example, a fund could invest in all the companies that make up the Dow Jones Industrial Average. Rather than trying to buy all those stocks yourself, and having to maintain them actively, you could buy shares in the fund. Doing so would allow you to grow your investment based on the performance of the Dow. The value of the funds themselves fluctuates and can be used as an investment or to realize profits. Mutual funds and exchange-traded funds have a lot of similarities, but also some very important differences. Mutual funds are closely "managed," and fees are charged as a result. Exchange traded funds are loosely managed and trade as shares of stock. We will be talking about funds in detail later in the book.

Retirement accounts

Most people are in the markets via retirement accounts. These are specialized accounts designed by Congress in order to encourage people to save money for retirement. The most common type of retirement account is called a 401k and is offered by employers, who will match investment funds that you direct to the account out of your paycheck. Typically, people don't play much of an active role in managing them. You can also create an individual retirement account or IRA. There are specific rules used by the IRS that govern retirement accounts, and the amount of money you can put in an IRA every year is strictly regulated, so that really isn't in the scope of this book, which is about directly managed to invest.

Investment success stories and market gurus

Investing in the stock market, if done correctly, can yield high profits. This can happen across a wide variety of time scales. For example, if you had invested $10,000 in Amazon in 1997, today it would be worth $1 million. Of course, we are benefiting from hindsight, at least to a degree. Nobody knew how dominant Amazon would become in 1997, but it was clear that Amazon was going to be a disruptor. It also shows what relatively small investments can achieve given enough time and growth.

Let's look at some specific examples.

Julie Rains turned $6,000 into $35,000 over a two-year period, purchasing shares of stock in Nvidia.

Anne Scheiber opened a $5,000 investing account with Merryl Lynch. By 1995 when she passed away, that account was worth $22 million.

While his path isn't advisable to follow because of its high risk, Tim Grittani turned a $1,500 investment into $128,000 by trading penny stocks.

Bob Brinker

For 34 years, Bob Brinker graced the airwaves with a radio talk show about investing. Although Bob has retired from his radio show, you can still visit his website and learn about his investment strategies. Brinker emphasizes long term investing with market timing and dollar cost averaging. He has developed three winning stock portfolios that you can follow in order to reach your investment goals. You can subscribe to his investment newsletter at http://www.bobbrinker.com

Tasty Trade

Beginning investors can learn a lot by following the podcasts from Tasty Trade. You will learn more about stock trading, day trading, options trading, and more than you will from most people. If you want to manage your own stock market investing, then tasty trade is the place to visit. The company is associated with a broker named Tasty Works. You can also use them as a broker, and they have the ability to do practice trading.

https://www.tastytrade.com/tt/shows/ryan-beef/

https://www.tastytrade.com/tt/learn/

Ric Edelman

Ric Edelman is another financial advisor who ventured onto the radio, he has a weekly radio show that airs on Saturday evenings in most markets. Edelman is well known as a very successful investor. He also runs an active investment firm. Ric Edelman really knows what he's doing, but keep in mind that he is motivated to win clients for his investment firm. You can get more info about that here:

https://www.edelmanfinancialengines.com/

Jeremy Siegel

Jeremy Siegal is a professor of Finance at the famed Wharton Business School. He is an advocate of investing in stocks. You can read his opinions on his website, and he often appears on the financial network CNBC.

https://fnce.wharton.upenn.edu/profile/siegel/

Squak Box

This is a daily TV program that runs in the mornings on CNBC. It's a famous stop for many business titans. Market conditions and predictions are frequently discussed.

Jim Cramer

Jim Cramer and his show "mad money" is one of the most famous investors in the minds of the public.

Chapter 2

Choosing a Brokerage

These days, selecting a brokerage is easier than ever, and at the same time more difficult than ever. What do we mean by this? Brokers are all around. You can find multiple brokerages on the internet, including many old stalwarts like Charles Schwab, Fidelity Investments, and Merrill Lynch (which has since been bought by Bank of America, now known as Merrill Edge for self-directed trading). TD Ameritrade has been in business since 1971, and E*Trade, which seems very much a part of the internet boom, was actually founded in 1981.

More recent entries into the world of stockbrokers include Tasty Trade and Robinhood. Robinhood is unique in that it's entirely based on a mobile app, and it offers commission-free trades.

There are many others, and frankly, it's impossible to list them all and all the alternatives. Ease of use can be an issue as well, and Robinhood probably takes the cake with that if you are comfortable using a mobile app to execute your trades (many others offer the ability to trade with apps as well, including tasty works).

Minimum Account Size

The first factor you might consider when just starting out is how much capital, if any, does the broker require you to have in order to open an account. Some might have a minimum amount of cash that you must put in to open an account like $1,000. Some brokers don't require any cash on hand at all to open an account, but of course, in order to actually buy any stocks, you are going to need to deposit money in your account. Typically, online brokers will have lower minimums than older, more established brokers. For example, Interactive Brokers, Tasty Works, and Robinhood have no minimum requirements.

Withdrawal Fees

Many of the considerations when you select a broker are going to depend on what type of trader or investor you intend to be. If you are looking to make short term trades that seek to profit in cash from the trades, then you are more than likely going to want to opt for a firm that has the lowest fees. On the other hand, if you are a long term buy and hold investor, then fees and commissions aren't going to bother you as much. With this in mind, be aware that some brokers may have withdrawal fees. If you plan on pulling a lot of cash out of your account that might eat into your profits.

Commissions

Day traders, swing traders and options traders might have concerns about commissions because you're going to be trading frequently and high commissions can eat into your profits. These days low commission brokers are available and you can even try Robinhood for zero commissions. In contrast, TD Ameritrade is known for having high commissions. Of course, competition from no commission firms is forcing some of the others to offer deals; for example, Charles Schwab is offering no-commission trades on many exchange-traded funds.

Analysis Tools

The more involved you are in an active trading life, the more analysis tools you are going to want to have available at your fingertips. Many companies offer a full suite of analysis tools, and it can be helpful to have them right on the screen when you are looking to make a buy or sell decision. Of course, you can get many analysis tools for free such as on Yahoo finance, and use them in conjunction with whatever broker you prefer for other reasons. One drawback of Robinhood is that it's got a pretty skeletal interface and although it's very easy to use to place your orders, it's lacking when it comes to analysis tools.

Margin Accounts

A margin account allows you to borrow from the broker in order to make a trade. When you have a margin account, you can borrow cash from the broker and use it to buy stocks or options, and other financial instruments. If you are looking to open a margin account, you will have to see what the requirements are for each broker you are interested in to determine whether they are a good fit. In order to open a margin account, the broker may require you to deposit more money. The amount of cash required to deposit to open a margin account will vary by broker.

Watch out for hidden fees

Be careful with other hidden fees that may not be so obvious as a withdrawal fee or commission.

Broker List

Below you will find a list of some of the most popular brokers:

Vanguard: https://investor.vanguard.com/home/

Tasty Works: https://tastyworks.com/

Robinhood: https://www.robinhood.com (to use, see app store)

Interactive Brokers:

https://www.interactivebrokers.com/en/home.php

E*Trade: https://us.etrade.com/

Ally Bank: https://www.ally.com/invest/self-directed-trading/

Merrill Edge: https://www.merrilledge.com

Fidelity Investments: https://www.fidelity.com/

Charles Schwab: https://www.schwab.com/

Chapter 3
Investing in Stocks

In this chapter, we are going to go over the basic concepts with regard to self-managed stock investing. In order to do it successfully, you'll have to be familiar with a lot of jargon and data that is used to evaluate the health of a company.

What are stocks

Let's be completely clear about what stocks are. When you buy a "share" of stock, you are buying a share in the ownership of the company. When you do this with your brothers' small business, you might end up owning a significant fraction of it like 20%. But when you are doing this with a publicly traded company, for most people you are buying a tiny stake in the company. Nonetheless, the stock is a financial instrument which represents an ownership share in the company. Theoretically at least, it also represents a claim on the company's profits (more about this later) and on its assets (should the company go bankrupt). Although most people aren't aware of it, there are two types of stock:

- Common Stock: This is what most people think of when you say "stock" and "stock market." A common stock gives you an ownership stake in the company, and if it pays dividends, you get dividend payments. You also get shareholder voting rights. That's for real, but it's up to you to exercise that right if they offer it.

- Preferred Stock: This is a less common type of stock that offers a different set of rights. One of the main differences is that preferred stockholders get priority claim on assets of the company if it declares bankruptcy. Preferred stock can also offer a dividend payment. We won't be discussing it because most ordinary investors are not buying preferred stock.

Aligning buying choices with your goals

The first thing you should do before investing in the stock market is to sit down and figure out what your goals are when it comes to investing. Everyone has their own goals, but here are some common themes:

- Build up a nest egg for retirement.
- Build enough wealth and passive income that you can quit work early or basically do what you want (live life on passive income).
- Make midterm (3-5 year) profits off the stock market.
- Make money now. So, you're looking to buy and sell stocks to get cash this year.

The first thing that we'll note about this is that if you are looking to make money now, then that means you're looking to be a trader or speculator rather than an investor. There are multiple routes to do this, but the main ones are day trading, swing trading, and options trading. We will explore these approaches in chapter 4. Keep in mind that there is a trade-off of risk and reward, the more you want quicker rewards from the stock market, generally speaking, the higher the risk, although the risks with options and swing trading can be mitigated.

If you are hoping to make midterm profits, then you are going to be looking at building a more aggressive portfolio. For those looking to build wealth and passive income, you may be looking at investing in stocks that pay dividends, investing in bonds, or using your stock holdings to generate income by selling options. We will discuss all of these approaches as we go on.

The last goal, building a nest egg for retirement, is a popular way that people look at stocks. In this case, you're looking for solid buys and using a "buy and hold" strategy, so that you build up a significant portfolio by the time you retire that you can slowly draw on at that time for income without having to keep working. We will discuss many of the strategies that can be used for this type of investing in chapter 5.

Aggressive vs. Conservative Investing

No matter what your strategy is outside of being a trader, you can also look at investing from another angle, which is aggressive vs. conservative approaches. And actually, there are two ways to look at this. The first is dividing your investments between stocks and bonds/money in a way that reflects whether or not you are after aggressive growth or trying to protect our capital. By money, we mean a wider array of products such as money market funds, CDs, etc. With bonds, your principal is (at least in theory) protected. The expectation is that under most circumstances, the stock market is higher risk but will grow your capital at a much higher rate than other types of investments. Of course, sometimes there are unusual circumstances, like the mid-1970s in the United States when the stock market was languishing and interest rates were sky-high. But most of the time, that isn't the situation.

So, if you are conservative, that is you don't want much risk to your capital, then you are going to put more money in proportion towards bonds, money market funds, and CDs that protect your principal, and a lower relative fraction toward the stock market. Financial advisors recommend that people do certain percentages based on their age, so the closer you get to retirement, the more conservative you should get with your investments. That way, you can protect your principal moving into your retirement years. The theory here is that if there is a significant stock market crash, your certain items in your portfolio go belly up, you would need time to recover from the losses. Younger people have time to do so, while those nearing retirement or in retirement don't have time.

The way that you distribute your investments among different types of securities for these reasons is referred to as asset allocation.

Financial advisors have a simple rule of thumb they use in order to suggest what type of asset allocation that you use. You take your age and subtract from 100, and then you put that proportion into stocks. So, if you are 45 years old, 100-45 =55, so you would invest 55% of your money in stocks and 45% in bonds and other more conservative investments.

In recent decades, they have gotten less conservative in asset allocation recommendations. Some advisors use 110, and there are others who even use 120. So, if we were using 120 and you were 45 years old, the proportion of your investment capital that should be in the stock market should be 120-45 = 75%.

The reason that financial advisors have become more relaxed about this is people are living longer and healthier lives, and many people now work past the age of 65.

Midcap, Smallcap, Largecap

Another way that you can determine the relative risk of your portfolio is by what types of companies you invest in. The first main characteristics that you can consider our market capitalization. A rule of thumb (that doesn't always apply) is that larger market capitalization means more stability and less growth, while less market capitalization means less stability but more potential for growth. Obviously, on average, smaller companies have more potential for growth, and some of them are going to grow by massive amounts and become tomorrows blue-chip companies. Just 15 years ago, Facebook was nowhere to be seen, and Amazon and Google were much smaller in comparison to what they are today. However, you can see that this is no more than a rule of thumb, as Amazon and Google, for example, are very large corporations now and yet still capable of explosive growth. Apple also saw remarkable growth over the past decade, even though it was relatively older.

It's pretty difficult to know what companies are going to grow from small cap to blue chip if you picked Amazon 20 years ago well then you were pretty lucky. Most of us don't have a crystal ball. However, as we'll see, you can use exchange-traded funds to get a basket of stocks instead of trying to pick winners and losers.

To calculate market capitalization, you multiply the total number of shares by the price per share. Let's imagine a fictitious company. If they are trading at $100 a share and they have 2,561,780 shares, then the market capitalization is given by:

$100 x 2,561,780 = $256,178,000

So, it's easy to calculate, and even better you can probably simply look up the market capitalization of any company. What category the company falls in is defined in the following way:

- Nanocap ($50 million or less): These are small companies that could be very high-risk investments, but also with a huge amount of potential for growth. You would need to do a lot of research before investing in a company this size, and should probably limit your investment since it might go bankrupt fairly easily.
- Microcap (Above $50 million but under $250 million): Less risky than nanocap stocks, but still pretty risky. On the other hand, lots of potential for growth, and looking a little more stable.
- Smallcap (Above $250 million, but below $1 billion) These are high-growth potential stocks for growing companies that have become more stable than the microcaps. Still a lot of risks, however. You can invest in

many smallcap funds so that you're not betting on one company.

- Midcap ($1 billion to $10 billion): Now we are getting into a good "mid-range" area, that gives you reduced risk that still has some growth potential. Of course, the growth potential may depend on what market the company is in. The *reason* the company is midcap may be its industry.

- Largecap ($10 billion to $50 billion): If you are conservative investor, then you're going to be investing most of your funds in largecap companies. This is the old "blue-chip" category.

- Ultracap (Market capitalization greater than $50 billion): Rather than extending the largecap category, those who control such things invented an entirely new category for the Amazon's and Apple's of the world.

A financial advisor will typically suggest putting more capital into midcap, largecap, and ultracap companies if you are a more conservative investor, and less capital into smallcap and the other smaller companies. It is the general perception that the largecap companies are stronger companies that can weather downturns in their industry and recessions. It's also believed that large, older companies are more stable.

However, if the 2008 financial crash taught you anything, one lesson you might take from it is that this isn't always true. Many companies got into big trouble in the 2008 financial crisis, and some of them were very well-established firms. Consider that GM, which has been a "blue chip" company for decades, had to be bailed out by the government. Bear Sterns, an investment bank, literally went under overnight despite being more than 100 years old. Its stock dropped by more than $100 a share over a short time period. Other large companies like Bank of America needed to be financially propped up.

So, while the advice given is generally true, it's not always true. If you are looking to run a self-directed investing account, you are going to have to spend a lot of time studying and decide for yourself what is high risk and what isn't.

One key strategy that can always help protect your capital is diversification. That doesn't just mean investing in more than one stock; it can also mean mixing things up among largecap, smallcap, etc. That way, you can take advantage of some of the growth potentials without risking everything in one area.

Volatility and Beta

Now let's start looking at some markers that you can look at in order to evaluate whether an individual stock is something you want to invest in. The concept of volatility is based in common sense. If you see a stock price swinging up and down rapidly over a short time period, to relatively high and low values, then it's highly volatile.

All stock prices move up and down a lot, that's why stock charts are choppy looking. But one that swings up and down with smaller magnitudes in price changes and does it at a slower pace, is less volatile.

But you don't have to eyeball a chart and try to guess. Instead, you should look up a quantity for each stock called *Beta*. This is a measure of the volatility of the stock as compared to the entire stock market as a whole. What Beta tells you is if the stock is more volatile than the stock market as a whole, or less volatile than the stock market as a whole. A stock with higher volatility is going to have a Beta greater than 1. A stock with less volatility will have a Beta less than 1. If a stock had a Beta of 1.75, that would mean its volatility was 75% higher than the market average. If it was 0.15, then it would be only 15% as volatile as the market. Let's look at a few examples (just jump on Yahoo Finance to look at your own, note they may be subject to change):

- Netflix: 1.49
- Tesla: - 0.39
- Apple: 0.89
- Amazon: 1.74
- Ford Motor Company: 0.91

Notice that Beta for Tesla is negative. What this means is that the stock has been moving opposite to the market as a whole. So, when the stock market goes up, Telsa tends to go down, and when the stock market goes down, Tesla tends to go up. The magnitude of Beta for Tesla is 0.39, so it's less than 1. That tells us even though it got contrarian movement, it's less volatile than the market as a whole.

Netflix meanwhile has a positive Beta, meaning it moves up and down with the overall market (at least right now). It's 1.49, so it's 49% more volatile than the market average.

PE Ratio

This is a price to earnings ratio. It gives you a measure of how the stock is priced relative to the actual earnings of the company. If a stock has an unusually high PE Ratio, that means its overpriced. In the actual formula, we use earnings per share or EPS. So, if a company earned $500, and it had 100 shares of stock, its earnings per share would be $5. You don't have to worry about doing the calculations, sites with stock market data like Yahoo Finance have all these items listed for you. In any case, you can look at the formula one time so that you understand what you are looking at:

PE Ratio = share market price/earnings per share

So, if the share price for our hypothetical company was $15, then the PE ratio would be:

PE = $15/$5 = 3

Suppose that another company with 100 shares also earned $500, so has the same EPS of $5. But say its trading at $10. Then:

PE = $10/$5 = 2

Since it has everything else the same as the first company but the PE is lower, it's a better buy. So, the lesson to take home about PE is that a high PE indicates the stock is overpriced, while a low PE indicates the stock is a good buy – the company has the growth potential that hasn't yet been priced into the market shares of the stock. So, using our example, we'd expect the price of the second company's stock to rise from $10 to say $13, while the overpriced company might see its shares scale back in price to the same value.

Of course, in the real world, life isn't this simple, but its one metric you can use to find stocks that are good buys. In the real world, all things are never equal. On company that has a high PE might be there because although both companies have had similar earnings up to this point, that company may be releasing a hot new product soon that is going to change the world. So, you have to take it in context of other information.

Here are the PE ratios for the companies we looked at in the last section, for volatility:

- Netflix: 126.71
- Tesla: N/A
- Apple: 14.99
- Amazon: 76.66
- Ford Motor Company: 12.59

Tesla isn't making profits, so it doesn't have a PE ratio. Of course, people still invest because they believe in the product. Amazon and Netflix have pretty far out PE ratios, which could be a danger signal, but it also reveals investors expectations that these companies still have massive growth and profit potential. Apple has (at least for now) run its course with the iPhone, so its PE ratio is pretty modest by comparison, on par with that of Ford Motor Company.

You will have to actually learn about the company, what its product plans are and projected growth in order to make rational decisions about PE and EPS. Don't just go with the numbers.

Earnings per share are usually given on stock market sites as EPS right below PE.

Price to Book Ratio

Price to book ratio is denoted P/B. In order to calculate it, you need to know the book value of the company's assets and liabilities. So, we have:

Book value = Book value of assets – assets of liabilities

Price to book is then defined as:

P/B = Market capitalization/Book Value

If P/B is less than 1, it's considered low. However, that by itself might not be meaningful. It can indicate that the book value is overstated. Generally, a low P/B is probably a bad investment. It generally indicates that the company is not doing very well.

However, no rules are set in stone. You have to look at other factors that may be in play. For example, the company may be getting in shape to turn around. It might have spectacular products that haven't quite been realized (think Telsa), or it could have a new management team that can reverse the fortunes of the company (think Apple when Steve Jobs returned).

It's also important to check the P/B for the industry the company is in. Some companies happen to be in a sector that has low P/B values.

Other Data to Look at

Let's review some of the other information that you will find listed with a given stock.

- Previous Close: Share price the most recent time the market closed. Keep in mind that many securities trade after hours (overseas).
- Open: the opening share price on the most recent day of trading.
- Bid: The amount that buyers are willing to pay for a share. These are often displayed as a size. For Apple on today's date, I see the bid as 178.35 x 800. That means the buyer is willing to buy 800 shares for $178.35 a share.
- Ask: The price sellers are asking per share. For Apple on today's date, it's given as 178.48 x 2200. That means sellers want to unload 2200 shares at $178.48. To actually get a sale, you have to have a selling price at the bid or lower. Notice the imbalance in ask size and bid size. Since ask size is larger, this is an indication that (right now) more people are looking to get rid of Apple stock than there are people to buy it.
- Days range: the range from low to high in share price for that trading day.

- 52-week range: A measure of the range of share price for the past 52 weeks.
- Volume: Number of shares traded today.
- Average volume: Average number of shares traded in a given day.
- Market cap: the market capitalization for the company, total shares x share price.
- Earnings Date: Mark this one on your calendar and read up what people are saying about it beforehand. This is the next date the company will have an earnings call and give their previous quarters results.
- Ex-Dividend Date: The day before the record date, that is when dividends are paid. You have to own the stock before the ex-dividend date to receive the dividend payment. If you buy the stock on the ex-dividend date, the seller still receives the dividend payment.
- Yield: Annual Dividend Per Share/Price per share
- Forward dividend: Estimation of the dividend per share paid for the year as a percentage of the share price.
- 1-year target estimate: Analysts estimates of the future stock price.

Placing orders and Mitigating Risk

There are different ways that you can place an order when buying a share of stock. The basic way to do it is called a market order. A market order basically instructs the broker to buy or sell the stock now, at the current market price. For a sale to actually take place, the price you ask for the shares must be within the bid price of a buyer. Once you hit buy or sell, if it's a market order, then you're going to buy or sell the shares at the market price that is available at that instant. Most trades are market orders. Market orders generally execute very quickly, but if you have an asking price that is too high, it might delay a sale. I've experienced this and found that when I really wanted to get rid of something, I had to cancel the order and place a new one.

A limit order tells the broker to buy the stock at a specific price or higher. If the stock price doesn't reach the specified price, the limit order may not be executed. So, a limit order is a name the price order, but it won't necessarily execute.

For example, suppose that you want to buy a certain stock that is fluctuating around $100 a share. You can place a limit order to buy the stock if the price hits $99.50. If the price drops and hits $99.50, your order will be executed, and you'll buy the shares. However, if the price jumps to $102 and never comes back down, then your buy order will never be executed.

The concept of a limit order can be used as a way to mitigate risk. So, you can place an order to sell your shares if they drop to a certain level. Using the same example, if the share price dropped to $98 and you had a stop limit order on your shares set at that price, then your shares would automatically be sold.

You can actually set a long-term duration for a limit order, up to three months in length. So, if you are patient and want to wait for a specific price, that may be an option for you.

Most new traders simply use market orders.

Chapter 4

Day and Swing Trading

Now we are going to look at a short-term strategy used to earn cash in the here and now, rather than investing in companies for long term growth. These strategies take advantage of the short-term changes in the stock price in order to realize profits. There are really three ways you can do this, the other is options trading, but we are leaving that for a chapter of its own since it's a different animal. The two methods we will discuss here are:

- Day Trading: When you day trade, you buy and sell the same security on the same trading day. This is a highly regulated activity. A brokerage will determine that you are a day trader if you execute 4-day trades within any 5-business day period (that makes you a "Pattern Day Trader"). To be a day trader, most brokerages require you to have $25,000 in your account. There are a few firms that will let you day trade with small accounts, but they charge large commissions. As a result, those companies are used by new day traders without much capital to learn, but experienced traders use regular brokerages so that they can avoid the high fees.

- Swing Trading: this is a lower risk strategy. This is simply a buy-low and sell-high strategy that can last any time length you want but up to a maximum of a few months. A swing trader doesn't day trade, so at a minimum, a swing trader will hold an investment overnight. Swing trading is a much lower risk unless the company goes bankrupt or there is a huge recession (and hopefully you are doing your research so that you know what is possible) the stock is probably going to go higher than what you paid for it at some point in the near future. Since its lower risk, swing trading has no capital requirements.

Despite the differences, the techniques used are the same. Day trading is considered a high-risk activity, higher risk than swing trading, and much higher risk than normal stock investing. It's hard to say that swing trading is really that high risk as compared to buying shares of an individual stock for any purpose. If it's not profitable to sell, the swing trader can just hang on to the stock.

Goals and Risks

The goal of day traders and swing traders is to make cash profits. So, you can think of it as a *trading business* rather than acting as an investor. You are more concerned with the short-term fluctuations in stock price than you are with the long-term prospects of the company. For the day trader, they are looking at profiting off of price fluctuations that happen over the course of hours, minutes, and even seconds. A swing trader is looking to take advantage of price swings in the share price that occur over periods of days, weeks, or even several months.

One risk, especially with day trading, is that emotion will take hold. This can happen with positive and negative emotions. So, you might have too much fear of loss and get out too early, or you might get greedy and not sell when you should because you have dreams of the share price skyrocketing.

Another risk is new traders don't use standard methods of mitigating risk that can minimize loss of capital when your speculations go wrong. In the next section, we will discuss some techniques that can be used to help guard your account against massive losses. One problem is many people simply jump on and start trading without really knowing what is going on. Instead, you should take the time to invest in yourself and take some courses on day trading from professionals. A search online will reveal that there are many different courses available. Many come with stock market simulators that you can practice with the learn the art of day or swing trading.

Potential gains

Most new day traders will probably lose money, at least at first. However, if you've put the time in to study and done some practice, including taking a course, you might be on the way to becoming a successful day trader. Those that are successful can make high annual incomes.

Risk Mitigating Steps

Before we review the techniques used to evaluate moves on the stock market, let's look at some important risk-mitigating steps you must take in order to successfully day trade without losing all your capital.

Clear Sell Criteria

If you are looking to profit off the rise in a stock price, then have a specific target in mind and sell when it reaches the target. Let's say you buy shares of a given stock at $10 a share, and it starts rising. You set a profit target at $15 a share. When it hits that you sell it and book your profits, and you don't let emotion get the best of you and fret if it does up to $20 a share. A greedy trader or one who gets overly excited might hold the stock too long, hoping it will just keep rising. But then suddenly it might drop back down to even a lower level than what they paid for it. You should have a profit target in mind when you buy your shares and stick to it no matter what happens.

Stop Loss Order

A lot of new traders don't put in stop loss orders. Use the 1% rule (don't risk more than 1% of your total account value on one trade) to set the level for your stop loss order. What a stop loss order does, is it automatically puts a sell order for your shares if the price drops to a certain value or less. So, if you buy shares of stock at $16 a share, you can put a stop loss order at $15. Then if the stock price drops to $15, your shares are automatically sold, limiting your total loss to $1 a share. If it continues dropping to say $7 a share, you can see how you've saved yourself a huge amount of grief.

Putting a daily limit

You can also help protect yourself by putting a daily limit on the amount of capital you're willing to risk each day. So maybe you only allow yourself to buy $3,000 worth of shares (or whatever) so that you're not betting the farm.

Avoid trading on the margin

Using margin trading (borrowing money from the broker) is where a lot of people get themselves into financial trouble. If you don't spend what you don't have, then you can avoid getting in trouble in the first place. Instead of letting yourself get emotional about some supposedly "sure thing", have a steady plan for profits that you earn over the course of time, rather than hoping that you've "found the big thing" and you're going to possibly get yourself in huge trouble by borrowing a lot of money to realize your dreams, when the odds are solid your predictions will be wrong.

Calculating risk

Let's look at how advisors recommend you calculate your risk. The risk on a single trade should be 1% of the capital in your account. Let's say that shares of a given stock are trading at $100 and you have an account with $50,000. So, 1% of $50,000 is $500. That means the most you can risk is $500, but that doesn't apply to the total amount spent on buying the shares, so you don't buy $500 worth of shares. What it means is that you put a stop loss order to limit your total loss to $500. So, if you put a stop loss order at $99, that is a $1 loss per share, so you could buy 500 shares. So, you could risk your entire $50,0000 account on the trade! But with the stop loss, if the stock starts tanking, you'd automatically sell at $99 a share, so you'd have $49,500 at the end of the day. Suppose it dropped to $75 a share. With the stop-loss order, it would have no impact on you. But if you didn't have the stop loss order, you would have lost $12,500 on the trade.

Candles

When people day or swing trade, they use "technical analysis" in order to estimate future moves of the stock. The only difference between the two trading styles is the time frames over which the analysis is done. A day trader might be looking at 5-minute intervals to determine what trades to make over the next few hours, while a swing trader might be looking over the course of a few weeks for big swings in stock price.

One tool that is used in the analysis is candles. You can see candles on any stock chart by selecting them as a display option, and you can also set the time duration. Candles were actually invented by Japanese rice traders. Markets are universal.

The candles have "wicks" sticking out from them. These indicate the high and low prices for the time period. Candles are red or green in color. A red candle indicates selling off is dominant, while a green color indicates buying is dominant. Or put another way red candle is associated with dropping stock prices, and green candles are associated with rising stock prices.

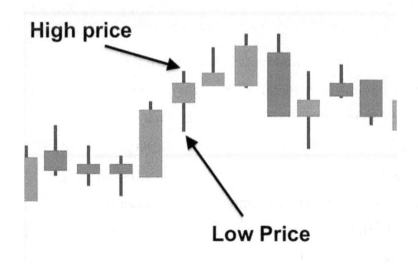

The top wick is the high share price for the period. The bottom wick is the low share price for the period. what the period depends on is what you select for the chart options. So, if you are looking at the chart with 5-minute intervals, the high and low prices indicate the high and low prices for each 5-minute interval.

The body is the solid block. If the block is green, then the top of the body is the closing price (time at the end of the time interval), and the bottom of the body is the opening price (price at the start of the time interval). For a red candle, it's the opposite, so the top is the opening price, and the bottom is the closing price. So, a red candle indicates the price dropped for the given time period; a green candle indicates the price rose over the given time period.

Traders use candles to estimate changes in the direction of the stock price. If a candle of one color engulfs the previous candle of the other color, that is its body is much larger in size, that can indicate a price reversal is coming. You can see it in the picture above, there is a red candle with a small body next to a green candle with a very large body, and that large green candle was followed by an increase in the share price. The large green body indicates that over that time interval, a large number of people bought shares of the stock, and increased demand means prices will be bid upwards.

A hammer is a candlestick with a small body and a long wick below it.

A green hammer at the bottom of a downtrend can indicate that stock prices are about to go higher. So that is a buy signal. If the hammer is upside down, it's called an inverted hammer or a shooting star, for a red candlestick. These occur at the tops of uptrends, and that indicates the stock price is about to begin dropping. A shooting star is a sell signal.

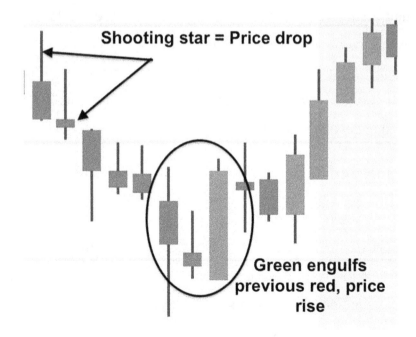

Shooting star = Price drop

Green engulfs previous red, price rise

Moving Averages

Another tool that is used in the analysis by traders is looking at moving averages. You can set the number of days (periods) over which you want the stock chart to display the moving average. Moving averages reduce the noise normally found in stock charts so that you can view price trends as smooth curves. Traders often look at charts with two moving averages, one a short-term moving average and one a long-term moving average. When the two moving averages cross each other, then movements in the stock price are expected to follow. You can use either simple moving averages, which is just the average of stock prices over a given period, or an exponential moving average, which is more sensitive to recent changes in price. When a short term moving average rises above the long-term moving average, then a rise in stock price is expected. The opposite occurs when the short term moving average drops below the long-term moving average. In that case, this indicates a coming decline in stock prices.

Support and Resistance

Traders look for signs of support and resistance in stock charts. Support occurs at the bottom of stock prices, while resistance occurs at the top of stock prices. Support is a price level that defines the floor for a given stock. That is the price never seems to drop below that value. Resistance is the ceiling for a given stock. So that price of the stock doesn't rise above that value.

Bollinger Bands

Bollinger bands use the standard deviation for the stock price to set levels of support and resistance for the share price. The upper Bollinger band represents a high price level that the share price is unlikely to exceed. Remember that we are talking about short term time periods here, this is for day trading or swing trading. The lower Bollinger band represents a price below which the stock is unlikely to drop. The width of the bands also gives us an idea of how much variability there is in the stock price. Below is a chart of Amazon with Bollinger bands. It shows that for the past six months, the stock price could not get above $1966.21.

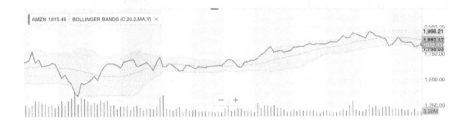

Bollinger bands are dynamic, so always change as the stock price moves. You can see how in recent months the bands for Amazon are much narrower, indicating that the price variability has dropped quite a bit, although if you look at the chart you'll note that the wide bands on the left are almost entirely due to the one decline in price that led up to Christmas eve 2018.

Summary

Day trading and swing trading are not for everyone, but they can be used to generate short term profits. Some people like the analysis and getting involved in the short term moves of the stock, so taking a very active role in trading. If the idea intrigues you but day trading seems too risky, consider swing trading, which really isn't that risky in comparison, but you should always use stop-loss orders and be ready to take profits when they come rather than holding too long hoping to get more profits. Also, it's possible to mix things up, and you can put some of your capital into long term investments and use other capital to fund some level of swing or day trading. As we will see later, people interested in short term profits in the stock market can also use options trading.

Chapter 5

Investment Strategies

Now that we have day trading out of the way, we are going to talk about some strategies that long-term investors use. The purpose of these strategies is to help you maximize potential profits that are made over the long term. However, we have to note before we get started that generally speaking, if you are in the stock market over the long term the odds are in your favor no matter what you do if you don't sell your shares. This is a good article that indicates how that would work. The author follows a hypothetical investor named Bob, who invests in the stock market only at stock market peaks. As the article shows, Bob still ends up with a million dollars:

https://awealthofcommonsense.com/2014/02/worlds-worst-market-timer/

That isn't to say that you should follow Bob's lead in your investing habits. Even though Bob ended up making a lot of money, he left a lot of money on the table too. To maximize your returns, you want to use sound investment strategies. But what's interesting is even during the Great Depression, the downturn wasn't forever. In 1933, the stock market increased by 67%. It also saw large gains during many other years of the depression, although it experienced a 33% drop in 1937, which was known as the "depression within the depression" when many of the gains that had been realized from 1933-36 were reversed, although that only lasted for about a year.

Let's look at the top strategies that you can use in order to ensure you do the most you can to come out without losses and that you maximize your returns.

Diversification

One of the most important investment strategies is diversification. It's the old advice, don't put all of your eggs in one basket. Diversification doesn't mean you can't follow your passions. If you have a company that you are really passionate about, by all means, invest in it. But you should limit the amount of capital that you put into any single company. There are not any hard and fast rules about this. You could put a limit of say 10%. So, if you are putting $2,000 a month into your investments, then only $200 can go to the hot new stock you think is going to increase as the years go by massively.

Remember one thing, that hindsight is 20/20 and far too many "sure things" ended up being duds.

Many financial advisors recommend that you diversify. In a self-directed account where you are picking your own stocks, you should also limit the number of companies that you invest in. The reason is that you need to know and study the companies that you pick. You shouldn't just be investing on a whim. You have to study the industry the company is involved with, the future prospects and estimates of analysts, and what the growth prospects of the company are going forward. Growth doesn't have to be huge; the economy grows with time, so even 'safe' investments are going to be worth a lot more 20 years from now, barring any major unforeseen events.

So, diversity when it comes to a self-directed investment account should take place along several lines. We have already talked about diversification by investing some money in large cap, mid cap, and small cap companies, etc. We've also discussed the way that many financial advisors propose that you protect your capital as you age by moving it more into bonds and other types of "safe" instruments. But we can do more.

Some other diversification strategies include putting some money into index funds as well as investing in specific companies. As we'll see in the chapter on ETFs, there is an endless number of ways that you can utilize ETFs in order to invest.

One way that you'll want to diversify is by investing in different sectors. For example, it would be foolish to put all of your money into social media companies, or by the same token put all of it into oil and gas companies. A good investor will invest in companies from multiple sectors. This will help you weather the ups and downs. When there are downturns in the economy, they are not going to impact every sector in the same way. Some sectors might even do well while the rest of the economy is languishing.

So, let's summarize the wide array of diversification strategies that you can use to help build a solid portfolio:

- Put some of your money in bonds, money market funds, and CDs to protect some of your capital.
- Buy stock in companies of different sizes. By some micro and smallcap stocks to add some growth potential. Buy some mid caps for solid but safer growth potential, and buy some large and ultracap stocks for added protection.
- Buy stock in companies that operate in different sectors. Invest in energy, health, finance, and other sectors.
- Use ETFs to add index funds and other investments to your portfolio.

Dollar Cost Averaging

Another strategy that is advocated by Bob Brinker and others is dollar cost averaging. We linked to an article at the beginning of the chapter where another "Bob" was described who only bought stocks during market peaks, but still ended up with $1.1

million in his account after 40 years. The thing to remember about "Bob" is he probably didn't end up with nearly as much cash as he could have had. The reason is he missed out on all the buy-low opportunities that were coming his way.

Now one thing to keep in mind is that it's virtually impossible to predict the direction of the stock market over a given time period of say a month or three months. One way to deal with this situation is to average out your buying of stocks as time passes. This is called dollar cost averaging. So sometimes you're going to be buying shares when stock prices are declining, and sometimes you're going to be buying shares when they are increasing.

One way you can do this is to invest a fixed amount of money each month without fail, and don't concern yourself with the short-term ups and downs in the market. If you are trying to build wealth over the long run, then the short-term ups and downs are irrelevant. Twenty years from now, is it going to matter if you bought Apple stock when it was $175 a share or $180 share? Spoiler alert: Probably not. What is going to matter is that you bought (say) ten shares of Apple every month without fail, so that after 20 years you owned 2,400 shares.

Someone who used dollar cost averaging would have ended up a lot better off than the "Bob" described in the article, and they might have been able to retire years earlier since our pal Bob had to wait 40 years to get his million dollars.

Growth Stocks

A growth stock is obviously a stock that is from a company that we expect to grow over time. However, when people talk about growth stocks, they are talking about solid, successful companies whose earnings are expected to increase as time goes on. A growth stock will have a high price to earnings ratio. Some examples of stocks that can be considered growth stocks are Amazon and Netflix. Although none of us have a crystal ball, it seems fairly obvious or at least likely that Amazon is not going anywhere, and it's likely to see increasing revenues for the foreseeable future. The same applies to Netflix, which has developed a service model that addicts its customers. Of course, in the world of capitalism, anything can happen, and five, ten, or twenty years from now, these companies might have been blindsided by the rise of more innovative rivals. But that remains to be seen – for now they are solid bets.

Growth stocks are less likely to pay dividends. That's because they are often companies that prefer to reinvest profits into expansion of the company.

The goal of investing in growth stocks is to take advantage of the future capital appreciation that you expect. So, you can buy shares of Netflix now for $360; maybe in five years, they are going to be worth $500 a share or more.

A growth stock should have the following attributes:

- It's a successful company and expecting to have increased earnings in the future.
- The Price to earnings ratio is high.
- The Price to Book ratio is high.
- If you are a dividend investor, you probably won't be investing in growth stocks.

The bottom line with growth stocks, is you are going to want to invest in more growth stocks if capital appreciation is one of your main goals. Of course, you can weight your portfolio, so maybe you only invest 65% or 70% in growth stocks.

Value Stocks

A value stock is a company with solid fundamentals, but lower stock prices, and the share price will be lower than expected based on earnings and other considerations. Since earnings may be high, but the share price is low, the P/E ratio will be low. Value stocks will also typically have a low price to book ratio. They may pay dividends and will have a high dividend yield.

If you are looking to build an income generating portfolio, value stocks are likely to be a part of your mix. Value investors often look for stocks that pay high dividend yields. A common strategy is to pick the companies that have the highest dividend yields among the companies on the Dow. Typically, an investor will choose 10 companies. They buy stock in these companies at the beginning of the year and hold them all year long. Then the following January they do the exercise again so that they always have investments in the 10 companies with the highest dividend yields on the Dow.

Other income investing strategies

Another income investing strategy that we will discuss later is to write covered call options. This is a way to divide up your shares into 100 share blocks and earn a monthly income of the shares. There is a risk you will have to sell the shares, however, and we will discuss that in the chapter on options.

Investing in bonds is also a solid income strategy when interest rates are high. A bond is similar to making a loan, except you're the lender. So, the borrower (which can be a corporation, a city, a state, a county government, or the U.S. government) will pay you interest. Bonds can also be traded on the bond markets.

Example Growth Portfolio

The main goal of a growth portfolio is to secure long-term growth. This can be done by carefully selecting companies that you believe have such long-term growth potential. If selecting individual companies, you should pick a minimum of 10 companies. You don't want to select too many because remember – you should be studying the companies that you invest in. So, if you bought stock in 30 companies, it might be hard to keep track of and make smart decisions.

Another approach would be to invest in growth-oriented ETFs, and we will discuss that in the next chapter.

A growth portfolio should have some protection in it. You don't want to throw all your money into Amazon, Netflix, Tesla, etc. no matter how good they look right now. There is always a chance that the market will tank and who knows, maybe world war 3 is around the corner.

So, in order to protect yourself, you should also put some money into bonds and a smaller amount into cash investments (those are money market funds, CDs, etc.). Suggested asset allocation for a growth portfolio could be:

- 75% in a diversified portfolio of growth stocks.
- 20% in bonds.
- 5% in cash investments.

Aggressive Growth Portfolio

If you are looking to build an aggressive growth portfolio, you can do it by adding some smaller companies with growth potential to the mix. You can even include international stocks from developing countries, that might have a huge growth potential over the next decade or two but also carry high risk. If you are looking for aggressive growth, you also probably don't want to be putting money into bonds and cash. Here is a suggested aggressive growth portfolio:

- 40% in a diversified portfolio of growth stocks (large companies)
- 20 % in a smallcap fund
- 20% in developing countries stocks
- 10% in a midcap fund
- 10% in micro and nano companies

Value Portfolio

If you are interested in a value portfolio that will have lower growth potential but more income potential through dividend payments, pick companies from the Dow that have high yield dividends.

- Invest 70% in value stocks.
- Invest 30% in bonds.

Please note that these portfolios are merely suggestions and do not constitute financial advice.

How often to buy shares

How often you buy shares to build out your portfolio is up to you and depends strictly on your personal situation and tastes. Of course, the main factor is going to be your access to capital to buy shares. There is no reason obsessing on it but you can buy shares whenever you want to. The organization takes precedence, however, and it's a good idea to schedule regular stock purchases on some kind of calendar. You can do it once a week, once every two weeks, or once a month. It should be at least once a month.

So, if you are using a dollar cost averaging strategy, you are going to buy a few shares of the same securities on a regular basis. For example, if Exxon is in your portfolio, you can buy 2 shares every 2 weeks. That doesn't sound like much but consider that after a year you've got 52 shares, and then after ten years you'd have 520 shares. Of course, if you have more capital to buy more shares, then do so. But you should never invest more than you can afford, only buy more shares when you've paid all your personal bills and other expenses.

Rebalancing

One of the most important concepts when managing your own portfolio is rebalancing. Simply put, this is a way to reallocate your investments to meet a given target allocation. So if you had an investment portfolio where you wanted 55% in high growth stocks, 25% in the S & P 500 through an exchange-traded fund, and 20% in bonds, every so often you would check to see the value of all your investments and see if they continued to meet your goals. Chances are they won't ;)

So, in that case, you'll have to use rebalancing. So, what you do is add up the current value of each investment portion, and then you buy and sell to get the portfolio back to the asset allocation that you want. Selling shares that you need to sell to rebalance is going to give the opportunity to realize some profits.

It is generally recommended that you rebalance once per year. You don't really need to do it more frequently than that.

Chapter 6
Exchange Traded Funds

Exchange traded funds, or ETFs as they are often called, are a very exciting way to invest in the stock market. There are many advantages to an ETF as opposed to buying individual stocks. You can use exchange-traded funds to track major stock indexes, such as the Dow Jones Industrial Average, the S & P 500, smallcap stocks, midcap stocks, largecap stocks, growth funds, value funds, real estate, gold, stocks in developing markets – you name it, it can be tracked with an ETF.

Essentially exchange-traded funds are like mutual funds, but they trade like stocks. So, you can just buy and sell shares the same way you'd buy and sell shares of Apple or Facebook. Unlike mutual funds, they are not actively managed by a financial guru so the fees are much lower. Also, while mutual funds only trade once a day, exchange-traded funds trade throughout the day like stocks because they are stocks.

ETFs Offer Automatic Diversity

When you invest in ETFs, you can choose between different indexes and sectors, among other things. So, you get automatic diversity because the fund is investing across a wide array of companies on your behalf. One of the most popular ETFs that are out there is SPY, which is a fund that has invested in the companies that make up the S & P 500. Imagine the difficulty you would have investing in all 500 companies, and then having to adjust the portfolio looking to weight the fund to get more money invested into companies that performed better, and then taking companies in and out of your investments as the makeup of the S & P 500 changed. Of course, this would be a complete nightmare. So why not let someone else handle all of that for you? You can just invest in that fund and then let the market do the rest.

There are exchange-traded funds for many different sectors and investment goals. Finding the right ones for your situation will require a bit of research.

The Main Companies offering ETFs

There are many investment firms that offer exchange-traded funds, but the main ones that you should spend your time looking at include:

- State Street SPDR
- iShares
- Vanguard

While you are going to find that these companies offer funds that cover many of the same sectors and indexes of the markets, you are going to want to go head to head comparisons. Two funds that invest in the Dow Jones Industrial Average are not going to give you the same returns, for example. The reason is that while they are invested in the same companies, the weightings of the investments may be different. So, fund A may invest in companies 1,2,3, & 4 by putting 25% of the fund in each company, but fund B might put 30% in company1, 40% in company 2, 15% in company 3, and 15% in company 4. Why would they do that? They might believe that companies 1 & 2 have much better growth potential.

So how are you going to find out which fund is better? By studying their past performance. Compare returns for different funds against each other and pick the one that you feel is best. Many times, the differences won't be stark. You will also want to have a look at fees associated with each fund, but for those coming from mutual funds you will be pleasantly surprised, the fees associated with exchange-traded funds are negligible.

Use Exchange Traded Funds to invest in ... everything

One of the things about exchange-traded funds is that you can put money into virtually anything. This makes them exciting and can offer an opportunity to build a real diversified portfolio but only by using stocks. For example, you can buy shares of VGIT, an exchange-traded fund offered by Vanguard. This fund invests in intermediate-term Treasuries – U.S. government issued bonds. So rather than buying the bonds themselves, you can buy shares in this fund.

GLD is a fund offered by SPDR that invests in gold. So, you can invest in gold, but do it by owning shares of GLD, rather than going out and buying gold itself.

Let's take a look at funds that can help you build a diversified portfolio that suits your investment goals.

Remember – these are stocks

Although we are mentioning funds offered by different companies, you don't have to go to that company to invest. So, while you could open a Vanguard account, you don't have to. These funds all have stock tickers, you can just log into your brokerage account and simply buy shares in whatever fund you like.

A look at some example funds

For examples of largecap funds, we'll have a look at offerings from Vanguard. Stock ticker VIG is a dividend appreciation fund. It tracks the "Dividend Achievers Select Index" on NASDAQ.

VUG, on the other hand, is a largecap fund that tracks growth stocks. The ten largest holdings in this fund include Microsoft,

Apple, Amazon, Alphabet (Google), Facebook, VISA, Mastercard, Home Depot, Boeing, and Comcast. Notice that by investing in this fund, you're automatically exposed to these ten companies while only having to make one investment.

When you look at each fund, you can also look at the weighting the fund has by sector. For example, this Vanguard fund has 34.9% invested in technology, 20% in consumer services, and 13.9% in industrials.

Different funds that cover the same general goal will have different weightings by sector and different companies in their portfolios, although there may be a lot of overlap. These differences will impact the performance of each fund.

VTV is another largecap offering by Vanguard. It is listed as a largecap value fund. The holdings in this fund are quite different, reflecting the different goals of the fund. This time the top 10 holdings are: Berkshire Hathaway, JP Morgan Chase, Johnson & Johnson, Exxon Mobile, Proctor & Gamble, Bank of America, Cisco Systems, Pfizer, and Intel.

VOT is a midcap growth fund managed by Vanguard. The holdings on this fund include Roper Technologies, Red Hat, and Twitter, among others. Vanguard considers it to be in their highest risk category, but if you are looking to add more aggressive growth to your portfolio, its an option to consider as opposed to making the investments yourself. Vanguard also has a few smallcap funds. You can also invest in microcap ETFs, IWC is a microcap fund offered by iShares.

Tracking index funds is one of the best ways to use ETFs. We've already mentioned SPY, but there are many other stock indexes that you can track to invest in different areas. Some of the other index funds and sectors you can track with ETFs are:

- NASDAQ Composite Index: Mostly technology stocks traded on NASDAQ.
- Wilshire 5000: Designed to track the entire stock market. Not as popular as SPY.
- S & P Midcap 400, Russell MidCap, Wilshire US Midcap: Track midcap companies.
- Russell 2000: Tracks smallcap companies.
- Sector funds: Track energy, healthcare, finance, utilities, etc.
- Emerging markets.
- Real estate.
- Corporate bonds, including junk bonds.
- Precious metals, including gold and silver.

ETFS and Dividends

One question many people have does ETFs pay dividends. The answer is yes, they do. So, if you are looking for a way to build an income investment portfolio based on dividends, exchange-traded funds can be part of that process. Dividends are paid out quarterly. The proportion of dividends you receive will depend on what percentage of the fund you own. So, if you own 0.1% of the fund, you will receive 0.1% of the dividends.

ETFs and Bonds

We will discuss this in the next chapter, but we are going to mention here that you can use ETFs to invest in bonds, but more importantly, you do receive any interest payments from the bonds.

ETFs Make it Easy

One of the nice things about using ETFs to build a diversified portfolio hitting different market capitalizations, sectors and so forth, is that you can diversify your portfolio without having to study the details on dozens of stocks and companies. Of course, different things appeal to different people; some people actually want to put the time in studying companies and their performance, while others will prefer the hands-off nature of ETFs.

What I like to do is mix it up, so I will invest 50% in individual stocks, and the other 50% of my stock market investing goes to ETFs. There is no reason to be exclusive one way or another unless you really want to.

Chapter 7

Bonds

Bonds are an interesting financial instrument that has been around for centuries. As we mentioned earlier, they were originally used by local Italian governments to raise funds. In those days, they were perpetual, so you would give your principle to the government and then receive interest payments for life. Maybe they could be thought of as the oldest annuities instead.

Later, bonds were issued with maturity dates as they are today. That is the date when the bond expires and you're supposed to get your money back, and the interest payments stop. A bond that doesn't mature is irredeemable. A bond is redeemed when you turn it in to get your principal back.

Bonds have traditionally been a "safe" investment used by investors to protect their capital. You can also trade bonds on the bond markets, and profit from changes in bond prices that happen when interest rates go up and down. We will be discussing how all this works below.

Bond Basics

Let's get started by talking about the basic concepts behind a bond and the basic characteristics that all bonds have regardless of who or what is issuing the bond. The first thing to know about a bond is that it's a loan that you make to the organization in question that issues the bond. In return for the money (the principal) that you provide to the bond issuer, they will make regular interest payments to you for the life of the bond, although as we will see, there are other ways to make this arrangement. Therefore, when you buy a bond, you are a creditor the same way that a bank is a creditor when they loan someone money to buy a car or to do home improvements.

Since a bond is a loan, it is formally known as debt security. Since bonds can be bought and sold on secondary markets, we say that they are negotiable. Bond prices fluctuate up and down inversely with interest rates. We'll see why below, and we'll also look at some examples of changing bond prices and try to understand why the prices change the way that they do.

Even though you can buy bonds from and hence issue debt to a company, a bond does not entitle you to an ownership stake in the company. It's only a loan to the company, but you have no rights regarding the company unless it goes bankrupt, in which case you'd have a claim on its assets. If a company does go bankrupt, by common law bondholders have priority over those who own stock in being repaid. In the table below, we compare some of the basic properties of stocks and bonds, so that you're familiar with the differences:

	Stocks	Bonds
Stake in company	Ownership (Equity)	Creditor
Defined Term	Perpetual	Until maturity date
Priority in Bankruptcy	Last	Before stockholders, after secured creditors

Who Issues Bonds

Bonds are issued by many different types of institutions. Corporations issue bonds. The United States government (and other governments) issue bonds. State, country, and city governments also issue bonds. Indeed, some of the most popular bands in the 20th century were municipal bonds, or "munis," which offer a tax shelter. They were often used by the wealthy to park money during eras of high tax rates so that they could avoid paying them.

Definitions

Now, let's familiarize ourselves with some of the important definitions that are associated with bonds. These definitions will help you understand how bond trading operates and help you to buy bonds if you decide you want to do that as a part of your investing strategy.

Par Value/Principal

The par value is the same as the principal. This is also called the nominal value. A bond is issued as a sheet of paper that has a value printed on it, which is the par value. It's also called the face value. So, when a bond sells for the first time, if the par value is $10,000, then you have to pay $10,000 to get the bond. However, it called the nominal value or face value because, on the markets, bond values change. So, if you decide to sell the bond on the secondary market, you might get more than $10,000 for the bond, or you might get less than $10,000 for the bond depending on what conditions dictate. When the term of the bond comes to an end, you will be paid back the face value. As we will see when we discuss U.S. Treasuries, some bonds work a little bit differently.

Coupon

The word coupon is used because of its historical legacy. The coupon is the interest rate for the bond. In the old days, bonds were actually issued with coupons that you could tear off and take in to receive your interest payment. Interest payments can be made with different frequencies depending on the issuer of the bond, however, the interest payments for most bonds are either paid twice a year or annually.

Clean Price and Dirty Price

The clean price is the price of the bond minus accrued interest. The dirty price of a bond is the price of the bond, including the accrued interest.

Yield

Yield is the return an investor can expect from owning the bond. If you simply buy the bond from the issuer and hold it, then the yield will be just the interest rate or coupon of the bond. Current yield is given by the annual interest payment/price of the bond x 100. Bond prices and yields move opposite one another. So, the higher the yield, the lower the bond price. The higher the bond price, the lower the yield. This will make more sense later.

A more complex calculation that is often considered is yield to maturity. That calculation takes into account the difference in the price that you paid for the bond as compared to its par value, the number of years until maturity, and the interest rate of the bond.

Redeem a Bond

This means to turn it in to receive your principal back, and interest payments cease.

Maturity Date

The date the bond expires, so the date is redeemed.

Callable Bonds

A bond can be called. That means that when the issuing entity calls the bond, it has to be redeemed and essentially the bonds life has come to an end at a date of the issuing entities choosing, prior to the maturity date. That means you get your principal back and interest payments stop.

The Health of Issuing Entity

While the interest rates paid by bonds are influenced by the overall interest rates, they are also influenced by the financial health of the entity that issues the bond. This is the same principle at work that you find when an individual goes for a loan. A person with good credit can get a loan with low interest rates. A person with bad credit has to accept a loan with high interest rates. The same thing happens in the case of bonds. If a company with a checkered history is raising capital by selling bonds, then it must offer high-interest rates. The lowest quality bonds are known as "junk bonds." Like a loan to a person with a bad credit history, they carry more risk, and there is some risk that you could lose your principal. However, some investors are willing to assume that risk for the high-interest payments.

Zero Coupon Bonds

This is a different kind of bond that pays no interest. Instead of paying regular interest payments, the bond will be sold at a price that is lower than the face value. However, when you redeem the bond, you are paid the face value of the bond. So, for example, suppose you buy a $100 zero coupon bond with a 6% interest rate. You will actually pay $94 for the bond. Then in 12 months when you redeem the bond, you get paid $100.

How Bond Prices Vary

The basic rule for bond trading is that when interest rates rise, bond prices drop. They do so because the higher interest rates will be available by purchasing new bonds, so the old bonds have less appeal. On the other hand, if interest rates drop, bond prices rise. In that case, the older bonds that paid higher interest are more valuable than the new bonds.

So, let's say that you purchase a $10,000 bond, and the interest rate is 6%. If the interest rate drops to 4%, what is the price of the bond if you try and sell it on the secondary market? In that case, the interest rate dropped, so the bond price is going to rise. The interest payment is $600. To estimate the new bond price, we take the price that would be paying $600 at 4% interest. That would be:

$600/0.04 = $15,000

Now consider an alternative scenario. If the interest rate rises to 7%, then the bond price will drop. It will drop in such a way that the price paid to buy the bond on the secondary market would work out so that $600 is 7% interest. So, the new bond price is:

$600/0.07 = $8,571.43

When the bond reaches maturity, the face value of the bond is returned. So, if you bought the bond on the secondary market for $8,571.43, and you got the $600 interest payments, you'd make a little profit when the bond reached maturity, and you get the $10,000 principal.

Municipal Bonds

Municipal bonds are issued by state and local governments to help fund operations, like building new streets or libraries. Short term municipal bonds have maturity dates 1-3 years from the date of issue, but most municipal bonds are long term, expiring in a decade or more. They have been attractive to wealthy investors because they provide a way to earn long term interest payments. The interest is usually not subject to Federal income tax, so historically they have provided a ready-made tax shelter. When top tax rates were 90%, you could avoid paying them by investing in municipal bonds. There are two types of municipal bonds. General obligation bonds are used for day-to-day operations. They are "backed" by the taxing authority of the government entity that issues the bonds.

Revenue bonds are not backed by the taxing authority of the government, but rather from revenue that might be generated from a given project. For example, if the government in question issues the bonds to help build a new highway, they can collect revenue using tolls.

You can invest in bonds online by checking out brokers that specialize in bond trading. You can also invest in corporate bonds issued by large companies like Apple and IBM.

United States Treasuries

Perhaps the most famous bands of all are those issued by the federal government. At least until now, these have been considered the safest investments in the world. The debt of the U.S. government keeps rising, and at this point, investors don't seem to be bothered, but at some point, bonds issued by the U.S. government may be less appealing, which would lead to a rise in interest rates paid by the government.

You may have heard about U.S. Savings Bonds. Interest from US savings bonds is tax-free for local and state taxes. They are non-negotiable, meaning that they cannot be traded on secondary markets. Since they are not tradable, the value of the savings bond does not change with time as interest rates change, the way regular bond prices can. Savings bonds are a type of zero-coupon bond, so they do not pay interest payments, and the maturity is 15-30 years. However, you can redeem the bond if you've held it at least 12 months. When you redeem the bond, you are paid the face value plus interest. However, you are penalized if you redeem the bond early, and the final three months of interest will be withheld.

Savings bonds are priced from $25 up to $10,000. To either buy or redeem a US Savings Bond, you go to the Treasury Direct website run by the federal government.

If you are looking for a short-term investment via the United States government, then you can consider Treasury bills. These have terms lasting from a few weeks up to one year. Just like savings bonds, they are zero coupon bonds so you will not receive interest payments. In the case of treasury bills, they are sold at a discount. Then when you redeem the bond, you get paid the full-face value. The difference between the discounted price you bought the bond for and the face value payment is the interest.

A Treasury note is an intermediate-term bond. They have maturity dates that range from 2 years up to 10 years. Unlike savings bonds and Treasury bills, Treasury Notes pay interest. The interest payments are paid every six months until the maturity date. At that point, you can redeem the bond and receive your principal back.

Finally, there are Treasury bonds. These are long term investments with a maturity date that can be 30 years. They also pay interest every six months. If you live long enough to redeem the bond, you can receive your principal back.

Corporate Bonds

Investors can also look at corporate bonds. They will pay higher interest rates than government issued bonds because they are higher risk. You can buy corporate bonds from a broker, the way you can stocks. The issues at hand in choosing which bonds to buy are similar even though the investments themselves are quite different. So, you will want to take time to review the company's fundamentals before investing in their bond offerings. There may be additional information to consider, such as how good the company is at handling credit. Just like you have a credit rating, bonds are rated as to their quality, which in a nutshell can mean how much risk there is that you'll lose your principal. As we noted earlier, the riskier the debtor, the higher the interest rate. High-risk corporate bonds can pay handsome interest rates and are known as junk bonds.

Buying Bonds Through Funds

You can buy bonds directly, but one of the easiest ways to get in the bond market is to invest using exchange-traded funds or mutual funds. As with stocks, diversification with bonds is just as important. If some company is issuing bonds that have a junk rating, you might fantasize about putting all your money in to get the 9% interest rates they are paying so you can have a nice income without having to work, but if the company goes bankrupt or simply doesn't pay the principal back, well then you've lost some money. You can protect yourself with diversification and buying into a fund that invests in bonds on your behalf is the best and safest way to do that. A bond ETF holds investments in bonds, but they trade like a stock on the stock exchange. Maturity dates won't be your concern, because the managers of the fund take care of the underlying assets on your behalf. One interesting feature of a bond ETF is that you still receive the interest payments. But even more to the point, you get interested payments each and every single month. Remember that bonds typically pay interest either once every six months or once a year. The good thing is bonds all have their own date when the interest is paid, so when you invest in a fund that contains a large number of bonds, they are distributed throughout the year, so you will get monthly interest payments. This can make investing in bonds via a fund more attractive. You can use bond ETFs and mutual funds to invest in every type of bond, from municipal bonds to corporate bonds and also US government bonds. If you go through an ETF or mutual fund, you can save yourself the headache of having to trade on the bond markets. Your fees will also be much lower.

Chapter 8

Mutual Funds

A mutual fund is a pooled fund of money from multiple investors that is used to purchase assets on their behalf. Mutual funds invest in many different areas, such as stock market indexes, different sectors, large cap, small cap, etc. You can also find mutual funds that are structured for growth or value and to meet the many different investment goals that people have, such as investing in bonds. In some ways, mutual funds are like exchange-traded funds. One important difference is that mutual funds don't trade on the stock market. Mutual funds are only traded once at the close of each business day.

Benefits of Mutual Funds

Like exchange-traded funds, one of the benefits of mutual funds is that they provide a ready-made way to have diversified investments. This will help to mitigate your investment risk. Mutual funds can be very highly diversified; some may hold hundreds if not thousands of investments in underlying assets. So, you get huge diversity when you invest in a mutual fund, however, remember that you will get the same diversity when you invest in an exchange-traded fund, and there are several advantages to taking that route.

Another advantage of mutual funds is you can find funds that are set up for your investment goals ahead of time. So, for investors that don't want to think about what they are doing, using mutual funds is a conservative approach to investing that is basically a set it and forget it approach.

Minimum Investments

If you are going to invest in an exchange-traded fund, you can buy as little as a single share to get started. This isn't the case with mutual funds. They are going to require a minimum investment. The required minimum investment isn't going to be very large, but will be at least $1,000 and can range as high as $5,000.

Fees

The fees for mutual funds can be relatively high, and besides the way that they are traded, this is one of the biggest arguments against them. A "load fee" is charged every time you buy or "redeem" shares of the fund. You don't sell shares of a mutual fund, you redeem them, that gives them back to the company that manages the mutual fund. Load fees can be quite large, going as high as 8%. That is huge when you consider the practically nonexistent fees of exchange-traded funds. Moreover, load fees can be complicated. There are front-end load fees charged when you buy the shares, and back-end load fees charged when you redeem shares. Back-end load fees can be variable, depending on how long you held the shares. The longer you hold the shares, the lower the fee. So, they are encouraging you to stay in the fund.

There are also "level-load" fees that are charged once per year.

Actively Managed vs. Passively Managed Funds

Funds can be actively or passively managed. A passively managed fund is typically one that tracks a stock market index like the S & P 500. Passively managed funds, as you might guess, charge lower fees than actively managed funds. The goal of a passively managed fund is to match the return of the index that the fund tracks.

Actively managed funds mean exactly what the name says; they have an active manager or managers that run the investment portfolio. As you might imagine, that costs money. The fund managers will buy and sell assets in the fund in an attempt to beat the average return of the stock market. So, they are doing what you would be doing yourself if you manage your own stock portfolio. Generally speaking, beating the average return of the stock market is not an easy task. However, some research exists showing that actively managed funds often beat the market. That said, they don't beat it by huge amounts, and the massive fees that mutual funds require can wipe out any gains from having the fund actively managed. Long term studies that have been done actually show that passively managed funds return nearly three times as much as actively managed funds.

Exchange Traded Funds vs. Mutual Funds

If you enjoy dressing up in a suit and going to an office to hand over your money to pay fees, and then let the professional manage your investment account for the next 30 years, then mutual funds might just be right up your alley. All joking aside, mutual funds are suitable for some people and not suitable for others. If you are the kind of person who has an interest in actively managing your stock investments, then you are probably not going to be someone who is interested in mutual funds.

The bottom line is that in reality, exchange-traded funds basically offer the advantages of mutual funds but without the constraints and extra fees. Mutual funds are a bit of hassle when compared to exchange-traded funds. As we mentioned above, long term studies at best (from the perspective of mutual funds) don't beat passively managed funds, and in fact, 30-year studies have shown much better returns from passively managed funds. Even if we accept that many mutual funds can beat the market, you have to ask yourself if it's worth paying all those extra fees in order to get active management.

With exchange traded funds, you're in complete control. You can trade day to day if you want to, and you don't have to pay any "back end" fees if you want to sell your shares. So, exchange-traded funds offer the diversity, convenience, and ability to invest in many different sectors and types of investments in one package, but they are far more flexible. When you are investing in exchange-traded funds, you are in complete control and don't have to worry about some mutual fund company. But most importantly, you don't have to pay for all the high fees. There are fees associated with exchange-traded funds, but they are trivial. There used to be less difference when commissions were more of an issue, and so you'd be looking at paying the broker a commission for trading an ETF. But for example, you can trade commission free on Robinhood. And outside Robinhood, many brokers are offering commission-free trades on ETFs. So that negates that old argument.

Problems Buying and Selling

Since mutual funds only trade once per day after market close, this can cause issues if you want to buy and sell shares. Suppose it's in the middle of the day and the S & P 500 is really moving. So, you want to buy shares in SPY. It trades like a stock, so you just pull out your smartphone and buy the shares. You see the price right there when you place your order.

In the same scenario with a mutual fund, if you decide in the middle of the day that you want to buy shares of an S & P 500 mutual fund, you will know what the price was the previous day. However, you can't know what price you're going to pay for the shares if you placed an order at that moment because the fund is not going to trade until after market close. That is a huge disadvantage.

Chapter 9

Options Trading

In this chapter, we're going to take a look at the exciting world of options.

One option is a contract that is based on some underlying shares of stock. Basically, an option gives you the right to buy or sell shares. There are two types of options contracts called calls and puts based on whether the buyer of the option has the right to buy or sell the shares.

These can be used to make profits based on the short term moves of stock prices. The good thing about options pricing is that options are much cheaper than the shares of stock that they represent. For that reason, if some people are interested in getting into short term trading, options are a good way to do it. So, whereas you would spend tens of thousands of dollars hoping to profit off a rise in stock price doing day trading, you can get into options and only spend a few hundred dollars and gain some profits off the rise in the underlying share price. The ROI for options contracts is much higher than it is for stocks.

Another way that options are very interesting is for income investors. In that case, you're going to want to use your shares of stock together with the options in order to generate income from your shares of stock. As we get into the chapter, we will see how that works.

Two Types of Options- Calls and Puts

So, let's get started by defining the two types of options that there are. They are known as calls and puts. A call gives the buyer the right to buy 100 shares of stock. They don't have to do exercise that right in the real world, and it turns out that in most cases, traders don't actually exercise the rights. Options have a value of their own and people try to make money as options traders, and don't really want to own the stocks.

But let's not worry about that right now- let's just try to understand how these things work. We will get into the details of puts in a minute, but for now, just note that a put option gives the buyer the right to sell 100 shares of the underlying stock.

The first thing you need to know about options is it that they are temporary. Every options contract comes with an expiration date. If the terms of the contract are not exercised by the expiration date, the option simply expires worthless. This can be used to the advantage of income investors who are hoping to earn some regular monthly income off of their shares. You can write a call option and sell it, and there will be some risk that you will have to sell the shares underlying the contract, but the odds are that won't happen, and you can pocket the money you made selling the option.

So obviously if it just involves what we said so far it would be hard to see why options would be worth money. But there are two other important things you need to know about options. The first is when you buy an option, you agree on the price for the sale of the shares of stock at the time the contract was written. So, if I buy an option on January 2 and we agree at that time that the share price is going to be $100 if I exercise my right to buy, but when the option expires three weeks later, and the share price is $120, you still have to sell me those shares for $100.

So that is in part a motivation for people to buy options contracts.

There's another thing that we need to know about options. That is this. Each options contract represents 100 shares of stock. The shares of stock that are represented by the options contract are known in the industry as the *underlying*. Some people will describe options by saying that when you buy an options contract, you control the underlying shares. And they will note that you're able to control the underlying shares for a fraction of the cost as compared to what it would cost to actually purchase the shares on the market.

That is true as far as it goes. But the extent to which you actually control the shares of stock will depend on how much capital you have access to, in order to carry out the possible options that this contract calls for.

So earlier, we mentioned that a call option gives the buyer the right to buy the shares at a fixed price. The price per share that is agreed-upon in the contract is called the strike price.

So, let's say that we're talking about Amazon stock. It's priced very high. Let's just say for the sake of argument that it's $1800 a share which is pretty close to the actual value. So, you could buy an option contract for a lot less money. After all, a hundred shares at that price are going to run you $180,000. That is not something to sneeze at.

On the other hand, you could buy an option on Amazon for quite a bit less money - a tiny fraction of what the actual shares cost. Right now, I'm going to look up an option and get a price so we know what we're talking about for real. So, a June 7 option which is a call for $1837.50 (the strike price) is selling at $30.70.

But here's the deal. The price given is *per share*. So, the total price or should I say the actual price that you need to pay to buy the option is $3070. OK, that's not exactly bus fare, but one thing we can say about it is that it is a lot less than $180,000!

However, if we were talking about actually exercising the option, you would need to have the money to buy the shares at the strike price. So, in other words, to actually exercise the option you need to have $180,000 cash, or you need to be so good with the broker that they will let you buy the shares on margin (that borrows money to buy the shares).

Now we can't say that that's actually an impossibility. You have to ask what is the situation in which you would really exercise the option on a call. Keeping things simple, let's say that the share price of some stock is $100 a share. So, let's say that you buy a call option on the stock with the strike price of $102. Now let's say that the price jumps up to $110. So, you exercise your right, and you buy the shares.

So why would the broker possibly loan you money to buy the shares on margin? Well, the reason might be that you could sell the shares immediately once you got them in possession – you just turn around and sell them on the market for $110 per share.

So, you borrowed at $102 per share from the broker, and then you sell the shares for $110, you pay the broker the $102 per share back. So far then you made a profit on the sale of eight dollars a share.

Now maybe that would work out, or maybe it wouldn't, it would depend on other things such as how much did you pay to buy the option.

An option for a stock that cost $100 is going to be a lot cheaper than that option we considered for Amazon earlier. So, let's have a look and see how much one of those costs for some real stock. Picking a random example, I looked up American Express, which is trading around $118.37 per share at the time of writing. Looking at options that expire in one week, an $118 call is $1.02. So, it will cost you $102 since the price is for 100 shares.

So, it might be possible for you to make a profit of $100 per share stock under those scenarios that I mentioned of borrowing money to buy the shares. So, if we imagine that we were able to borrow the money, we would make an eight dollar per share profit, and then we would have to deduct the one dollar per share fee that we paid to buy the option in the first place. So, you would still end up making a profit.

But you always have to keep in mind that's not how most options end up. The fact of the matter is the vast majority of options are simply traded back-and-forth on the options markets. Investors are hoping to make profits on the trades, nothing more and nothing less. So, people invest in options, not for the point of actually buying the stock in most cases, instead, they buy options to make money off of trading the options themselves.

Options Pricing

So, to understand how this works you need to know how the pricing of options goes up and down. So, for right now are focused on calls. In this case, what happens is - if the share price goes *above* the strike price for a call, the general rule is that the call is going to go up in value.

If the strike price is above the share price, and the share price is dropping, in that case, the value of the call option is going to go down.

The price of an option is also affected by the time left until the option expires. More time left, more value. You can buy options that expire at many different dates. Some are weeklies meaning that they expire next week. You can also buy options that expire many weeks into the future or even months into the future, but they are more expensive. The reason they are more expensive is not only is there a long time before they expire but looking at it another way, there's a lot of time left for the stock to move that could really change the value of the option.

Then the share price is higher than the strike price of a call option, they say it "in the money." When the share price is equal to the strike price, it's "at the money." If the share price is below the strike price for a call option, it's "out of the money."

What you need to remember is the closer the option gets to the expiration date, the more it's price decays. There is a tug of war between the time decay of the price and the share price. So, at the same time if the price of the shares (in the case of a call option) is rising above the strike price, then the price is going to be rising.

For this level of the book, we're not going get into the actual formulas, but there are ways to predict the actual price. But a general rule of thumb you can keep in mind is that a dollar rises in the share price is going to lead to a $100 rise in the value of the option. That's because each share goes up a buck and it's 100 shares for the option.

Be advised this is far from exact, but it's a reasonable rule of thumb to understand what's going on. You can buy a more advanced treatment of focuses only on options to learn what the real formulas are and how they work. Also, if you get online, you can find spreadsheets which will do the calculations for you and the predicted prices are very accurate.

There is a parameter you need to know if you want a more accurate estimate of price changes, which is called Delta. Delta is something you can read on the stock info about the option provided on sites like Yahoo Finance. What it tells you are is a more accurate estimate of what the change in the option price is going to be for every dollar change in the share price.

So, if delta is .6, and the share price rises by one dollar, then the price of the option on a per share basis is going to raise $.60. That means the total price of the option would rise by $60. The value of the option that comes from the underlying stock is known as the intrinsic value.

The value of the option that comes from time left to expiration is called extrinsic value. At a certain point that will totally lose value. Compare two options, an option that has a longer time to expiration but the same strike price as another option will be worth more money.

Let's look at that for American Express. I quoted you an option that expires in a week for $118 and it was $1.02 per share. But if I took three weeks out an option with the same strike price costs twice as much money. The listed price is $2.05 per share. That reflects the fact that with three weeks left until expiration, that option will be around long enough to take advantage of any volatility in the price of American Express stock before it reaches the expiration date.

But of course, there's a balance - at some point, the time value is going to be decaying enough that it takes a lot of value away. So, you have to have a sense of when the best time is to buy and sell options.

When you are trading options, you need to stay on top of it very closely. I have found that in a matter of hours the money I invested has doubled, so if I had been paying attention, I wouldn't have been able to sell them and take advantage of the profits. In other cases, option prices can drop quite fast as well. So, if you remember our discussion from day trading one of the things you want to do as you want to use stop-loss orders. You can use pretty much everything that you use trading stocks when training options. So, you can make sure that you don't lose your shirt on options as well. But of course, that's the time we're talking about a few hundred dollars so you're not necessarily going to lose you lose your shirt, but you probably don't want to lose that money.

Summary of Call Options

Looking at it from the perspective of buying a call option, and trading call options here is the summary. The first thing is the price of the option is quoted on a per share basis. So that means if the price is listed at $2.05 since there are 100 shares for every options contract, one contract will cost you $205.

You can buy multiple contracts at once if you want to, just so you know.

Buying a call option means that you have the right to buy those 100 shares at the strike price, that will be your right, but it's optional. That's why they are called options.

You would only decide to buy the shares at the strike price if the market price of the stock rises above that strike price. So, in that case, you would be saving money by buying the shares using the options contract.

But always keep in mind the vast majority of options contracts are not exercised. People try to make money off of trading them.

As a trader, what you're looking for is a dollar rise in the underlying share price. Then you want to look at Delta, and note that when the stock price goes up by a dollar per share, the price of the option will go up in proportion by Delta. We can use another specific example. Suppose that delta was .5. This means that if the price of the stock went up a dollar, then the price of the option to go up to $.50 per share. In turn, that means that for 100 shares, the price of the option will go up to $50.

The last thing that you need to understand about buying call options is if the share price drops below the strike price, in that case, the option loses massive value. They aren't worthless, but they are cheaper by a lot. As you get closer to the expiration date, the price is going to plummet if the price of the shares is still below the strike price.

If the option expires and the price of the shares is still below the strike price - that option is completely worthless on the expiration date.

Now on the other hand if the price of the shares is higher than the strike price for a call option, in that case on the expiration date the difference between the share price and the strike price is going to be the value of the option. Soon the expiration date, if the share price was $104 and the strike price was $100, the call option would be worth four dollars a share for a total price of $400. Of course, you would have to find a buyer, and it would have to be somebody that wanted to exercise the option. Because after the expiration date an options contract can't be traded any longer.

Writing Covered Calls

Viewing this from the other side, now let's look at a strategy that an income investor can use with covered calls. As someone looking to make monthly income, in this case, we're talking about writing a call option.

It's known as a covered call because you use shares that you own to *cover* the option as a kind of collateral. So, going back to our fictitious stock that was $100 a share, you might write a call option if you're reasonably confident that the price of the stock is not going to go above a certain value.

After all, an option is only valid for a few weeks in many cases, so depending on the volatility of the stock, it might be worth the risk. As an example, you might write an option contract for $103 strike price. Then you could sell that option contract and the money paid to buy the option contract from you, it's called the premium.

You get to keep the premium no matter what.

So that can be some income, and there is a strategy of writing covered calls on a repeated basis to earn a regular income. And the more shares you have, the more options contracts you can write.

So, in the event that the option contract was exercised you wouldn't really lose out on anything. Well, I'm not being 100% honest, you would lose out on the missed opportunity of the rising price of the stock. So, say, for example, that the stock rose to $105 a share. So, you could have sold the shares for $105 a share, but because you wrote the options contract, you might be forced to sell them for the strike price of $103 a share. This means that you missed out on a two dollar per share profit.

However, you still made a profit. If you are using the shares to generate the income, you probably bought them a while back, so maybe you paid $95 a share for them say. So, if you sell them for

$103 per share, you still made a profit on the actual sales of the shares.

Plus, you got the profit from the premium. Going by the AMEX example, if you had sold the call option for $2, you add that to the strike price, and you're actually making $105 a share. Of course, this example is a little contrived, but whatever money you make from the premium can help make up the lost potential profits you could have made from simply selling the shares without getting involved in an options contract.

In short, as a writer of a covered call, there really is nothing to lose unless you're very desperate about holding onto those shares. And in that case, you probably would not be thinking about writing an option anyway.

Also, since you end up with profits, you can use that money to buy more shares of stock and maybe you will look at something else instead.

Now guess what happens if the share price drops. In that case, the option expires worthless. So, you get to keep the shares, and you get to keep the premium that was paid to buy the option contract. To sum up, if you write covered calls, you basically profit either way the stock moves. A covered call is a very good way to make some money off shares of stock that you own.

You just have to accept that there might be some risk you'll have to sell the shares of stocks. So, depending on what you have in your portfolio, this can be making you some pretty good profits off of premiums each and every month. Just remember that they may exercise the option but something like 80% of options are never exercised. But there will be times when the options are exercised. But chances are in the vast majority of the time you will be able to keep your premium and the shares of stock. You can also minimize the risk of having to sell by picking a good strike price. And if you have multiples of 100 shares of stock, you can write multiple options contracts based on them and generate a really nice monthly income.

Put Options

Now let's talk about put options. A put option is the opposite of a call option in the sense that you try to profit from a decline in the stock price. The buyer of a put option has the right to *sell* shares of stock to the writer of the options contract.

One reason that people buy put options is so that they can have an insurance policy on their stock. So, in other words, it's a way to protect against huge losses. So, let's say you buy stocks at $100 a share and the share price plummets. Just for the sake of an illustration, we'll say that it plummets to $20 a share. So, if you had done nothing, you would lose $80 a share. But on the other hand, if you had purchased a put option with the strike price of $95, even though the shares had plummeted, you would be able to sell your shares without much of a loss. They would be sold for $95 a share if you exercised your right on the option, and you would only lose five dollars per share.

Other people buy put options as a way to basically short the stock, so they are betting on profiting off a decline in the share price.

Note that in the case of put options, it's similar to that with call options in that people buy and sell the options just to make money off the trades. Therefore, most of the options are never exercised. However, if a put option expires in the money, there is always a risk that it will be exercised.

In the case of put options, they are going to make money when the share price drops. So that means if the share price drops below the strike price, then a put option becomes in the money. The reason is that the buyer of the put option would be able to sell the shares at a price that's higher than the market price. If the share price is equal to the strike price of a put option, we say that the put option is at the money.

Now let's look at the alternative scenario. Just like with call options, put options have an expiration date. If the share price is above the strike price of the put option at expiration, then the put option is basically worthless. So, if the expiration date is reached, we say that it's out of the money in that condition.

Hedging your bets

There are different types of trading strategies that people use to hedge their bets when they are trading options. So, you can buy call and put options simultaneously so that you can make money no matter which way the stock moves. Or if you're not that sophisticated, at least you can protect your losses. So, if you had bet wrong that the stock was going up but it actually went down and your call option was worthless if you priced a put option at the right straight price it would probably be in the money, and so you would make some profits from that instead.

There are many other strategies that can be used, they're very sophisticated, and beyond the scope of this book. Using those more advanced strategies will require training and experience and probably putting a lot of your effort into options themselves, which is probably not something long-term investors want to deal with. That said, you can make simple profits from trading options.

Chapter 10

Beginners Mistakes

Investing in the stock market can be exciting. It can also generate feelings of fear and despair. These emotional rollercoasters can lead new investors into making bad decisions. Many new investors also fail to educate themselves about how the markets work and the things they need to pay attention to. We all make mistakes, and these factors and more can lead to costly mistakes that lead to loss of capital. However, if you take some time to educate yourself and prepare ahead of time, you can minimize your mistakes and the costs of mistakes that you do make.

Prepare Before You Start Investing

Many people who decide they want to get into the stock market are anxious to do so. However, it's important to prepare before you start buying shares. The first thing that every person should do is make sure that they have an emergency fund of cash stashed away, and that you will not use it to buy stocks or to cover losses. The purpose of an emergency fund is to have money on hand in case you hit the skids with a job or lose other sources of income if you have a car or medical emergency, or your basement floods and you need to pay for expensive home repairs. Recent surveys have shown that far too many Americans have been neglecting basic savings, and many could not even meet a $400 emergency car repair. If you are in a situation where you couldn't pay for a $400 car repair, then you are not quite ready to get into the stock market. You should work to save up a little bit of money first. Many experts recommend that you save up around six months of required funds to pay all your living expenses, and that is good advice, however that doesn't mean you have to wait that long to start investing, but you should at least get two months ahead before you start buying stocks.

Another important part of preparation is education. And congratulations, by reading this book, you've demonstrated that you are the kind of person who is willing to take time to learn before jumping into something! That is a very important consideration, especially when money is involved. You should also look into courses that are available online and read as many books as possible, especially when trying to determine what kind of risks you are willing to take and how to marry your investment goals with that. There are many online courses available on basic stock investing, day trading, swing trading, options, and other topics. There are even many good videos you can watch on YouTube to get a grasp of many of the basic topics.

In recent years the development of simulators is one of the most exciting tools for education. These can be really useful, especially if you've never done self-directed investing before, but especially for those who are looking to be day traders, swing traders, or trade options. Practice makes perfect as they say, and that's as true with investing and trading as it is with anything else. If its important for a football player to practice before a game, its important for a new trader to practice day trading or options trading, before putting real money on the line.

Investing or Trading Based on Emotions Rather Than Facts

One problem with investing and trading are that emotions ride high. It's completely natural to experience emotional highs and lows as the stock market does its usual roller coaster ride. However, what you don't want to do is let emotions start guiding your decisions and taking you over.

The process of being guided by emotion can start at the very beginning when you choose your very first stock to invest in. Ask yourself a question – why are you choosing that particular company? Are you picking different companies because you think they are cool, or because you are really taking a cold hard look at company fundamentals? You should be selecting companies based on whether or not they meet your investment goals. So you should be looking at their earnings, their future prospects, the P/E ratio and other important metrics that will help you decide whether or not a company is 1) in good shape both now and for the long term future as far as you can see it, and 2) that the company actually helps you meet your investment goals.

Maybe you are in love with Apple. But being in love with Apple is not a good enough reason to buy stock in Apple. If Apple doesn't match up with your investment goals, you should be looking elsewhere.

Emotion has a huge influence when people are facing losses. People panic and sell off. When the Dow Jones starts declining, people start moving their cash into "safe" investments, many that these days don't even pay hardly anything like money market funds. Some people don't even do that and just sell out and take the cash.

As an investor, you need to be disciplined. The courses of action described in the last paragraph that is governed by fear and panic are not the courses of action that a disciplined investor is going to take. Now if you are a swing trader and the market is declining, then either you're going to sell, or you're going to be shorting the stock. If you are a long-time investor, however, you most certainly shouldn't follow the lemmings over the cliff. What you should be doing is looking at a downturn as a buying opportunity. So, you should be loading up on shares, but don't do it all at once. When the market enters a downturn, nobody can be sure how low it's going to go, so you want to make disciplined, periodic purchases the way you always do. Dollar cost averaging always works when you are in it for the long haul. That doesn't mean you won't miss some opportunities, but over time the market will rebound again, and by the time you are in your retirement years, the prices will be much higher than they were when you originally invested in most cases.

There are going to be some cases when you're going to want to bail. An individual stock can decline for many reasons, and sometimes there is a point of no return. For example, Bear Sterns crashed from $170 a share to $2 a share over a matter of a few weeks. If you had invested in Bear Sterns, then you should have been studying the situation closely and you would have gotten out early.

So, you might want to bail from an individual stock when the data tells you that this is the right course of action. But you never get out of any stock simply based on panic. Know what the fundamentals are of the company.

Emotion works the other way too. When it seems like a stock simply goes up and up, people can start getting giddy about it. You might be tempted to put your entire life savings into that one stock. But that is a bad idea, no matter how good the stock is. As we've mentioned before, it's great to know that Amazon increased so much that an investment of a few thousand would have made you a millionaire, but hindsight is 20/20. Right now, it's impossible to know which if any social media companies are going to actually bank profits and still be around in 20 years, so it would be foolish to put your life savings into one. The so-called investor who goes around claiming to know what the next sure thing is can be called nothing more than a fool.

Another problem is people get emotionally invested in one company. Maybe it's because of the mission of the company or the products it makes that people think are going to "change the world." But when you get emotionally invested in a company, you start becoming irrational. Good examples include Tesla and Theranos. Let's take the latter case. Theranos claimed to have invented a revolutionary means to let people test their blood and to have medications delivered. It became clear that it was a sham, but the people who were emotionally invested in the company and the female CEO were literally fooled about it – and some still are even though it's clear now that Theranos is done and the CEO may even be facing charges.

In the case of Tesla, the jury is still out. They make high-quality products but have problems with delivery and scaling. They may yet overcome those problems. But if you talk to many Tesla investors, they are zealots about it. If Tesla ends up going down the drain, many of the investors may go down with it. Is it worth it?

To avoid letting emotion take over whether you get swept up with the lemmings running off the cliff when there is a bear market, whether you panic when an individual stock starts dropping, or whether you get hyper-excited when your favorite company is booming, you need to have rules in place beforehand and follow them.

For example, one rule that you could have in place is you never invest more than 5% of your portfolio in any single company. If you do that, then you are not going to be damaged even if you're a bit taken in by the company or you panic when it drops – or worse – miss when you should get out. Think about the poor fools who stayed invested in Bear Sterns until the end, and even the government wouldn't bail them out.

This is one reason why I like ETFs, although you don't have to use them for your entire portfolio. They divorce you from the problems that can arise when you start getting emotionally invested in one stock.

Putting Too Much Stake in the past Performance

One mistake many new (and even experienced) investors make is putting to much credence in the past performance of a stock. The fact is, as they say in the disclaimer, past performance is not a guarantee of future returns.

So, people often look at past performance as a guarantee of future performance when history shows that it is more often than not, simply not true. So, you might've seen a run-up of some particular stock over the last year, maybe it was Netflix, or maybe it was Amazon. And so, you just expected to continue. Of course, the real world doesn't work that way and the expected returns may not materialize. As it is, although none of us can tell the future, the run-ups of Netflix and Amazon may have come to an end. Of course, over the very long term, we probably expect both of those to grow. We simply don't know, so putting all of your investments into Netflix isn't a good idea, but you might want to put some of your investments into Netflix.

So, let's take Apple as another example. Apple has had an incredible run up over the past 10 to 12 years. Ever since they introduced the first iPhone, growth has been spectacular, expectations have been high, and returns have been even better. We really haven't seen anything quite like it before.

Apple is still a solid company, but one thing you can say is that it has run into a stall. Right now, nobody is expecting Apple to make the huge leaps that it did for the past 12 years. You could've invested in Apple in 2014 say and simply expected the run-ups to continue. What you couldn't foresee is that Apple was running out of new inventions already back then. Without Steve Jobs at the helm, it's hard to see Apple rebounding and getting back to the spectacular growth experience that they had before. Of course, you never know, maybe they will bring in some new management that has some of the talents that Jobs did, and they will recover their lead. But before you invest, you should be tracking what the company is doing.

So, I hate to beat a dead horse, but this is one that needs to be beaten. I spent a lot of time talking about index funds, but a lot of times that advice will fall on deaf ears. People that want to have a self-directed investment fund find them boring.

Here are the facts. There are some investors that have a fantastic ability to pick individual stocks that are going to be winners. And it's fun doing it. As I said earlier, I don't want to discourage you from picking your own individual stocks. But like I also said I tend to put 50% of my investments in exchange-traded funds. The reality is that most people don't have all the time in the world to be studying companies, market trends, and the like in order to pick good stocks.

Now if you do follow my advice and limit yourself to picking maybe 10 stocks, then you're on the way toward more success. At least, under those circumstances, you don't have to spend 24 hours a day studying companies in the markets. However, broad index funds that give you approximately the same returns as the total Stock market, so they are a fantastic way to invest and build long term wealth. The answer is to follow both paths even if you use a different asset allocation than I have.

Diversifying, but Not Really Diversifying

So, you build your investment portfolio. And you come and tell me that you've decided to go with picking all individual stocks. And then you tell me that you've invested in 25 companies. Sounds fantastic! But then you tell me they're all banks.

Remember that when you diversify, that doesn't just mean picking different companies. It also means diversifying across sectors, company size, and even investing in different types of securities like bonds. You might even consider investing in different overseas markets, including Europe, Japan, China, and developing countries. Diversifying helps you weather storms that don't impact the entire economy but might hit one sector hard. At the time of writing, because of trade disputes, you might be in a world of hurt if you invested in soybeans, while the rest of the economy is humming along. Diversification is so important it should be mentioned often.

Lured by Penny Stocks

One of the mistakes the new investors make is they get pulled in by seemingly easy money opportunities like penny stocks. Although it seems like a great idea, i.e., you can buy tons of shares for hardly anything, it is definitely not a good idea. One of the problems with Penny stocks is although *some* people can make money at them, is that the industry is full of charlatans. They know the new investors are going to come along and they aren't really going to be aware of what Penny stocks are about or how to invest in them properly. So, these charlatans take advantage of the new investors by making it seem like you can make far more profits from penny stocks then you really can.

Since the stocks are so cheap, in many cases, fraudulent people will buy up tons of shares of the stock in order to drive up its price. When something is a dollar a share or at most five dollars a share, that's not that hard to do. Then after the price goes up, they can document this in some kind of product that they might be selling like an online video course about penny stocks, or there are a lot of newsletters that fly about (usually online). People looking for fast money who are ordinary people with real needs and good intentions, but they don't really know what's going on, are easily swayed by this kind of publications. I'm here to tell you right now, you should not give in and join the crowd. If you're planning to be an investor, there is absolutely no reason to even think about penny stocks at all. Maybe one in 1000 will actually turn out to be a viable company at some point. But picking out that one in 1000 is a fool's errand. If you're a new investor, it's highly unlikely that you're going to be the one that picks out the winning penny stock.

Remember also, the price of something upfront doesn't mean that it's really a bargain. So, buying a one-dollar stock might be as good as burning your money in the fireplace. Of course, we are all familiar with the problem of buying a used car, and you know that when you're buying a used car, a bargain price is not necessarily a good sign. Yes, you might save money buying the car up front, but when it breaks down in the boonies two weeks from now and needs a new transmission, well the price has suddenly gone up hasn't it?

The same phenomena are at work with the vast majority of penny stocks. So yes, you can get a penny stock at a bargain price. You can buy 1000 shares for $1000. Boy, that sounds good compared to Amazon where you can't even buy one share for $1000! Or Netflix, you might have two or three shares. The difference, of course, is that company that you bought your thousand shares in probably isn't going anywhere anytime soon, if ever.

There's a reason it's a penny stock isn't there?

So in the same way that you might be hurting yourself by buying a used car for $1000 that's going to break down on the road cause you trouble, and then require you to spend another $3000 to fix it, it's better buying a more expensive car where you pay upfront but you know it's reliable transportation.

If you were to invest in Netflix and only get those two shares, at least you would be making profits as they grew in value over the years instead of having thrown away $1000 on a pipe dream.

The bottom line with Penny stocks is don't go near them at all. In fact, I would advise that you don't even invest in micro caps, those are companies not ready for prime time. Yes, some of them might make the cut at some point, but your odds of picking the successful ones out are slim to none. Invest in real stocks, and that's where the real bargains are because they are going to grow in value over time. Something like Netflix, which is $360 a share now might be $500 a share in two years, or maybe even $1000 a share. I would call that the real bargain.

Are You an Investor, or a Trader?

The next big mistake made by beginners that we should address is not being clear if you want to be a trader or an investor. If you were going into this wanting to be an investor, you need to avoid the temptation of constantly trading stocks. Part of being an investor is choosing a solid investment from the get-go as much is that as possible, and then riding it out. That doesn't mean that you stick with it forever if it is not looking very good in the future at some point, but you have to give it a reasonable amount of time before bailing on the stock. And if you do decide to bail, do so not because of your gut feelings or because of a price drop which may be temporary, but because of the fundamentals and what they are telling you.

Remember that stocks are highly volatile over the short term. That short-term volatility can disguise a long-term upward trend. If the fundamentals and earnings of the company are good, there's no reason not to expect that future rise in price. So, you should be avoiding the temptations to dump the stock. Short term fluctuations or even stalls over a few months should be ignored. For example, if it isn't going anywhere over three months or something like that or even if it drops for a month or two, that isn't a reason to dump the stock.

Another thing that happens to people is they get excited about buying stock in a few great companies. Then they keep watching the market, and they notice that there are some other opportunities coming up – hey why didn't I invest in those?

So, they get really excited and they sell the stock in the original companies and buy shares in these other ones. That's not a good approach that you should follow. I would say that you've got to at least commit to something for at least a year. At the end of each year, you can evaluate your portfolio and see if there are some stocks that you want to get rid of it in exchange for others.

And remember again that I am advising that you have 50% of your portfolio in exchange-traded funds and they should be index funds like the S&P 500. You can invest in funds like that and then simply not even think about them anymore, accepting the fact that you keep investing. You should be buying new shares and doing it every single month, but other than that, don't touch them. Those are there for long-term growth.

If you find that you're really intrigued by constantly trading stocks, even though you've set out long-term investment goals, maybe the truth is you're more suited for being a trader. Remember this about trading - studies show that most day traders fail to make a profit. That shouldn't be that surprising. I don't know if you've heard of a little rule of thumb called the Pareto principle or not. It says that in any endeavor, 20% of the participants make 80% of the money.

It's probably worse than that when it comes to day trading.

No, I don't want to discourage you completely, but if you decide you want to be a day trader or a swing trader, I really encourage you to take a course. Some courses that are available cost a lot of money, and you might be looking at $1000 investment just for the class, but it's worth it and might save you tens of thousands later on. That's something I can guarantee you.

If you decide you want to be a day or swing trader, I have to say that I'm willing to bet a lot of money that those who take courses and prepare ahead of time outperform people who just jump on and start trading after reading a book.

So, you're probably going to want to be one of the people who take the course. It's an investment and it will be totally worth it. Some of the courses are taught by professional day traders who will actually work with you to make sure that you're learning the material.

Another suggestion that I have if you have goals of becoming a long-term investor, but you're intrigued by trading, is to take a small part of your capital that you have available for investing and instead of buying stocks with it, you buy and sell options. One reason to consider this is the fact that investing in options doesn't require as much capital to be invested. Remember you're talking hundreds of dollars at a time, while with day trading you might be talking $10,000 at a time, as we discussed in the chapter about it earlier. So, you can satisfy your urges to make short term profits by trading options with a small portion of your capital and then use most of your funds for long-term investing in stocks. That's a little bit safer than becoming a day trader and blowing all your money.

Getting Suckered by Gurus

Now let's look at another phenomenon that happens with regard to the stock market. Many people who are new to the industry end up trusting the wrong people. If you go online and there are endless marketers, courses, YouTube videos, and who knows what else applying for your attention, it's easy to fall prey to people that are peddling bad information. At the same time, there are lots of TV gurus dispensing advice about stocks. Of course, some of these are in financial shows and so forth but it can be hard to know what's right and what's not when you're just starting out. No, I'm not saying that all these people selling courses online or dispensing advice on television are fakes. Obviously, I wouldn't be saying that when I just advised you to look into a day trading course if you're considering day trading. There are some good people out there.

But it's hard to know who to listen to and who do not listen to. If you're going to be doing long-term trading, one person that I thoroughly trust and highly recommend is Bob Brinker. It's unfortunate for those of us still investing that he retired. But you should see if you can get podcasts of the many previous episodes of his show and just listen to them. In the show, he constantly dispensed his wisdom about stocks and he continually educated. You can also subscribe to his newsletter and sign up for market timer, and also look at the portfolios that he has set up as examples for different investment goals. In my view, there's no way that you can lose if you follow Bob Brinker for long-term investing.

Not Really Knowing Your Companies

One mistake the people often make when starting an investment career, is they fail to study the companies that they invest in carefully. We've already talked about choosing companies to invest in based on emotions rather than on the fundamentals. However, it needs to be emphasized that you also need to really know *what* the company is doing, how it's spending its research money, and what the long-term plans are for the company. You need to then look at whether or not those long-term plans are going to be viable for long-term profits. To gather all this information, the fact is you really need to study the companies very closely. Your investigations of each company need to be extremely thorough. That's one reason why diversifying by investing in say 50 different companies is probably not a good strategy. A range of 10 to 20 companies is far more realistic so that you can really understand where those companies are going. You also need to have a good handle on the leadership team at each company. Just reading a few brief articles about tweets that Elon Musk sent out is not good enough. You really need to know what he is doing what he's all about and the rest of his team that is leading the company.

Putting Money Where You Shouldn't Because of Financial Illiteracy

Let's face it, financial education in the United States isn't all that good, in fact, we could say in most places its non-existent. What we learn we get from our parents, other relatives, and maybe some friends. As a result, far too many of us aren't financially savvy and can be taken in by many different schemes. Some are more obvious than others, but one is annuities. If people actually understood how they worked, it's doubtful that anyone would really buy into one. And no, an annuity is not an investment. People's financial illiteracy also makes them susceptible to "it's the next best thing" claims. You should put your skeptic hat on when you hear that. We aren't saying that it never happens, but chances are something people are crowing about isn't really the next best thing. You are the key to fighting your own financial illiteracy. Keep learning. Take advantage of all the books that are out there, and sign up for courses if you find one directly related to the eventual investment path that you decide to take. If there are investment clubs in your area, consider joining one. With all the information that is available, there are plenty of options to choose from.

Biting off More Than You Can Chew

If you have never run a self-directed investment account before, then its probably not a good idea to jump in as a day trader. But many people catching the excitement bug, overreach when they start trading stocks. The cold reality of this is that you should gain some experience before you start working your way into more risky activities. You don't have to sit back in a sweater with a pipe and buy an endless array of mutual funds, but you might want to hold off for a while on the day trading. Slowly learning to buy and sell stocks is a good way to get started. You should stick to simple trades for 3-6 months before considering anything else, and secondly, you should make sure that you can afford to lose any capital that you put into more risky ventures. Remember that a day trader account has a minimum requirement (in most cases) of $25,000. Can you afford to lose $25,000? If the answer is yes, and you would still have a large sum of capital available for more conservative investments, then you might be ready to get started on your day trading career. However, if you are in a situation where losing $25,000 is going to be something that is very noticeable and painful, then you're probably not ready to day trade. But look at the other possibilities. For example, people who want to become more active traders seeking shorter-term profits should be looking at swing trading.

Not Reinvesting Dividends

If you are a beginner, you should reinvest your dividends until you've built up a significant portfolio. Many people do use dividends as a way to make a living, but if you are just starting out with your investing and you get a small dividend check that really isn't going to make a difference in your day to day life, you are probably better off reinvesting it. Grow your portfolio so that down the road, your dividend checks are so large you can live off the passive income.

Your Investments are Small

You should invest the maximum you can invest. Of course, that doesn't mean that you invest so much that you can't pay your utilities (I've been there). But you should invest adequate amounts. Otherwise you're not really going to get anywhere. Start with at least $500. You should live a more frugal life to make sure that you have more funds to invest. Your later self will thank you.

Not Having a Plan

Many new investors (and plenty of older experienced ones as well) don't have a firm plan in place. I advise that you start out by writing down your goals. Keep a journal. Make sure the investment goal you have in mind is clear. You should even be shooting for a specific amount of money over a given time period. So, work backward, think about how much money (realistically) you would like to have available at age 60. Then work out a plan that can help get you there. Of course, since the stock market is inherently unpredictable and who knows what could happen on the political front, there are no guarantees in life. But history shows that the stock market has been relatively stable for very long periods of time, and so planning for the future in a systematic way makes perfect sense. How well you actually stick to the plan you draw out is a personal decision you are going to have to deal with on your own.

Pulling out Too Early

There are two ways this can manifest itself. The first is the stock market starts crashing, you panic and pull your money out and put it in the bank – where it will earn next to nothing. The second way this can happen if you invest and make some gains, but then your mind starts wandering, and you get worried. You start thinking you better pull out now while you're ahead. Both paths are fundamentally flawed. Remember that over the long term, the stock market always goes up. So, pulling out during a crash is the wrong move as we've mentioned before. During a crash, you should be buying stocks, not thinking about pulling out. As far as the second possibility, remember that over the long term, those that stay the course are the ones that always win. So, unless you're doing swing trading, don't book any profits. Let your investments sit and focus on adding to them year after year, let the fruit ripen for a long time period.

Chapter 11

Individual Retirement Accounts

Another way you can consider investing as an individual is using an individual retirement account. These can be utilized in addition to the rest of your investment portfolio. There is no reason to take an either-or approach, in fact, both and all of the above is the correct answer. An individual retirement account or IRA, as its name implies, is something you set up on your own distinctly from your employer. So, an IRA is not like a 401k. Personally, I consider having an IRA as another form of diversification. It's not the main game in town, but its there and will be there in my retirement years.

One of the advantages of setting up an IRA is that you get certain tax protections. There are two main types of IRA's, and the way that they have tax protections is specialized for each type. So, one way you can set up an IRA is for tax-free growth of the investments. In the other case, it's a tax-deferred account.

Traditional IRA

If you set up a traditional IRA, the money is taxed when you withdraw it in retirement. So, there could be a little bit of risk. The United States government is in massive debt with problems with long term funding of social security, Medicare, and other problems. So how does anyone know what the tax rates are going to be in 10, 20, or 30 years? That is one risk to consider. However, the money in the account is allowed tax-free growth, and you can deduct your current contributions to the account from your taxes now.

Roth IRA

A Roth IRA involves after-tax contributions. So, you pay taxes on the money now, and then invest it in your account. Then it can grow tax-free and when you withdraw the money, it's tax-free. However, there are certain conditions that need to be satisfied in order to use a Roth IRA tax-free in this manner. A single person must earn less than $122,000 per year in order to contribute fully to a Roth IRA. For married couples, the cutoff is a household income of $189,000.

Contributions that you can make to an IRA are limited. For a Roth IRA, if you are under 50, you are allowed to contribute $6,000 per year. If you are over the age of 50, you can contribute an extra $1,000, which is used for "catch up" money, so someone over the age of 50 can contribute $7,000 per year.

If your income is too high to qualify for a Roth IRA, then you will have to use a traditional IRA, which means you'll be stuck paying taxes in the future no matter what they are, while your Roth buddies are rolling in the dough.

The government generously allows you to contribute to a traditional IRA up to 70 ½. You can take out distributions early, but if you are younger than 59 ½, there is a 10% tax penalty. Contributions for a traditional IRA have the same limits as a Roth.

The Bottom Line

An IRA offers a chance to build up another retirement account. You can buy IRA's through your broker. The small contribution amounts probably mean that for most investors, and IRA is not going to be their main mode of investment anyway. However, as I said in the introduction to this chapter, an IRA offers another safety valve, it can help to make sure that you don't wipe out all of your investment funds should things go wrong.

Chapter 12

Annuities

We conclude the book with a brief look at annuities. We are doing this for informational purposes because annuities are not investments. They are a kind of insurance. The idea behind an annuity is to guarantee a fixed income payment for life in retirement. As they are a kind of insurance, they are sold by insurance companies. This makes buying a good annuity a troubling prospect. Earnings from an annuity are taxed as regular income by the government.

You don't need to buy an annuity ahead of time. There are immediate annuities available. The way this works is that you pay the insurance company a one-time lump sum of money. In exchange, they guarantee you a fixed income stream the rest of your life. They also come with a death benefit.

You can also get a deferred annuity. Some of the rules of a deferred annuity are similar to those of IRAs. For example, if you buy a deferred annuity but opt to take payments before age 59 ½, you get a 10% tax penalty, which is the same rule for IRA withdrawals. In fact, the account used for a deferred annuity is basically a mutual fund, but the insurance company guarantees a fixed payout. You can even purchase an annuity inside an IRA. My advice is don't soil your IRA by doing that.

A deferred annuity also comes in with a built-in 7-year delay, so you can't pull out any funds until the seven years is up without paying heavy fines.

There are two major types of annuity contracts. A straight life policy will pay out based on life expectancy. The payments will continue even if they exceed the original amount paid in. However, if the beneficiary dies, the payments stop.

For life with period certain, there is a 10 or 20-year time limit built in. But a surviving beneficiary gets the payments until they run out.

Besides getting the fixed payments, you can make a withdrawal. A systematic withdrawal can be paid quarterly, semi-annually, or annually. You can also take a lump sum payment of the entire amount, which sounds like it basically erases the annuity.

Drawbacks

Annuities are often saddled with lots of fees and commissions. This basically leaves people who are naïve at a disadvantage, and the insurance salesman has a motivation to force people into annuity contracts. Large commissions can lead insurance salespeople to act in their own best interest rather than in the interest of the client. Also, the guarantee of the annuity is only as strong as the insurance company. If it folds, you don't get your payments. We all saw how strong big AIG was.

The idea of an annuity can be appealing for a lot of people, for the simple reason that the idea of regular, fixed payment to your bank account in old age sounds like security. However, you should look under the covers for this one. Generally speaking, you are better off simply putting your money elsewhere. Invest your money where it can grow and you can provide yourself with regular income payments in old age without having to have paid huge sales commissions to some insurance agent, only to be followed by hefty fees paid to the insurance company. With all the investment options available today, there really isn't any reason to consider an annuity.

Conclusion

Thank you for taking the time to read *Stock Market Investing for Beginners*! I hope that you found this book informative and enjoyable.

With the advent of the internet and other technologies, the stock market is more accessible to small investors than ever before. In this book, we've reviewed how to get into investing in stocks, bonds, options, ETFs, and mutual funds. The variety of ways that you can invest are seemingly endless but also offer unprecedented opportunities. I hope that readers will take advantage of them to grow their own wealth and do it the right way, carefully and over time.

You could simply set up an IRA or 401k and forget it, but managing your own portfolio is fun, interesting, and can lead to more returns both over the short-term and the long-term, allowing you to grow your wealth faster and to enjoy the fruits of your labors in your retirement. Of course, you may not ever actually retire, you may find yourself actively investing and trading in stocks to keep the money rolling in!

We've also covered trading strategies for the more ambitious, including day trading, swing trading, and options trading. These methods can be profitable, but please remember that they do carry extra risk. Follow the advice given in the book to minimize your risk as much as possible.

Remember that all investing carries risk, and despite following all the strategies described in this book, you may still lose money. The information we've provided here is for educational purposes only and does not constitute financial advice. Your own situation will be entirely unique. When you are unsure about an investment move, please consult a professional financial advisor.

If you have enjoyed this book, please drop by the book listing on Amazon and give us a sincere review. Thanks again for reading!